D0456909

FOR THE SENDER
Love Is (Not a Feeling)

◄——— music

words ———►

FOR THE SENDER
Love Is (Not a Feeling)

ALEX WOODARD

HAY HOUSE, INC.

Carlsbad, California • New York City

London • Sydney • Johannesburg

Vancouver • Hong Kong • New Delhi

Published and distributed in the United States by: Hay House, Inc.: www.hayhouse.com® • *Published and distributed in Australia by:* Hay House Australia Pty. Ltd.: www.hayhouse.com.au • *Published and distributed in the United Kingdom by:* Hay House UK, Ltd.: www.hayhouse.co.uk • *Published and distributed in the Republic of South Africa by:* Hay House SA (Pty), Ltd.: www.hayhouse.co.za • *Distributed in Canada by:* Raincoast Books: www.raincoast.com • *Published in India by:* Hay House Publishers India: www.hayhouse.co.in

Book design: Nena Anderson • *Photo contributors:* Alex Woodard, Caroline Woodham, Lee Sammartino, Dennis Anderson, Dan Hamilton, Scarlett Lewis, Patrick McClory • *Illustrations:* Jordan Pundik

Library of Congress Control Number: 2013950841

Hardcover ISBN: 978-1-4019-4123-9

17 16 15 14   4 3 2 1
1st edition, February 2014

Printed in the United States of America

SUSTAINABLE
FORESTRY
INITIATIVE

Certified Chain of Custody
Promoting Sustainable Forestry

www.sfiprogram.org
SFI-01268

SFI label applies to the text stock

Contents

DA CAPO (music)

to play from the beginning — It., da: from, capo: head.

"So when's the next one?"

The question came from behind me, where it hung in the air for a moment before trailing off into the emptying theater. I turned to see legendary songwriter Jack Temp-chin standing by himself in the middle of the worn-down wooden stage, looking into the curtain's dark, folded corners for an answer. I smiled and went back to watching the last of the crowd trickle out the front doors until Molly Jenson took me by the arm and said she wanted to keep on doing whatever this was.

But what was it?

We'd just performed a concert of songs we'd written about four moving, real-life letters I'd received over the last couple of years. Most of the audience members were leaving the theater with an album of these songs, enclosed in a small book called *For the Sender* that I'd had printed for the performance. I'd woven my own journey through the letters and songs, and as the project slowly came together the result read like a book, sounded like an album, and, after tonight's show, felt like a concert.

Up until that night, no one really knew what I was working on, not even the friends who had helped me write the songs. I wasn't sure myself at first, and when people would ask me I'd run through the same questions in my mind: *Is this a book? An album? A show about a book and album? All of the above?*

All I knew was that I felt as if I'd been holding this little bird in my hands, a sleeping ball of feather, waiting for the right time to spread her wings out in the world. And in front of two capacity crowds on that cold January night, I closed my eyes, opened my hands, and let her go, hoping she might fly.

She did fly, up through the aisle, out the dilapidated front doors of the theater, and into the clear winter sky, leaving Jack onstage wondering out loud what I was already thinking to myself: *When's the next one?*

Our question would soon be answered by a woman who'd been in the audience that night. But I didn't know this yet, so I packed up my guitar and left the theater, thinking this was probably the last time I'd see that little bird.

The year unfolded with new beginnings, and among other firsts, I got a horse. I thought she was just a simple, quiet trail horse, one of hundreds that change hands every day. I'd ridden her a couple of times and she seemed fine, but I didn't know as much as I thought I knew about horses. I found out later that she was the daughter of a two-time world champion and half sister to more champions than anyone who knew about these things could remember. And for an unfortunate reason I would soon discover, she was priced to sell.

My very first encounter with her should have sent me running for the hills, but she showed me something beautiful that day in a passing glance, and I took her home. Decisions based on passing glances aren't without risk, and it wasn't long before I found myself late one afternoon midair between her back and the ground, where I lay for a few anxious moments wondering if I was going to walk again. That's where our story begins.

And the little bird that flew out of the theater that night, the one I'd been holding in my hands, hoping she might fly? She crossed the sky a couple of times, traveling over mountains and streams and freeways, through rain and wind and snow, learning how to keep the air under her wings. Her spirit got stronger and her flight steadier, and she came back down to rest for a while.

You're holding her in your hands now.

The Dirt

THE DIRT

There is no end in nature,
but every end is a beginning . . .
and under every deep a lower deep opens.

— RALPH WALDO EMERSON

the horse

∪

I'm in a crumpled heap with a line of dirt as my horizon and four horse hooves as moons setting into an ocean of fine gravel and dust. My index and middle fingers are slow to respond to an anxious request for movement and after what seems to be an eternity locked in a few seconds they flutter up and down, like weather-beaten sails on a boat drifting across this earthen sea.

Set against the late-afternoon sky is a threatening storm of muscle and bone, a stocky body the color of sand framed by a flowing blond tail and mane. She is my connection to the ancient, my first steps into a world of deeper and more present being, and her quiet demeanor disguises a horse with more power than I know how to harness. I lay in the dirt and remember small, round Alberto, who works at the barn where I board her, watching her run in the pasture and saying in broken sentences *She more powerfullest horse anywhere I ever see, even if she not so big. That horse, she different.*

She bites me the first time I meet her at a four-thousand-acre cattle ranch east of San Diego. A friend is cinching up her saddle and I'm on the other side of her, stroking her neck gently, when from the corner of my eye I see her head begin to turn and before I can react she thrusts her half-open muzzle into my chest. Her bite doesn't break the skin but the impact is enough to send me back a couple of steps.

In the next breath time slows to a crawl and I see something else there in her eyes, something soft and vulnerable asking to come out. I see it and I believe it and with the passing of the lead rope from my friend's hand to mine, I take her with me.

I'm impatient to ride her after I bring her to the boarding facility near my house so I put a saddle on her and lead her into the riding arena. We're alone and I think I know what I'm doing but I don't and when I swing my leg over her back and press my calf against her flank, she raises her head high in the air and takes off like a building tempest across the dirt. As she accelerates into a turn at the end of the fence line, I launch off her back into an unmoving pile of bones and blood in the dust where I'm no longer sitting on a horse, hoping to connect with something more guttural than the cell phone in my pocket.

I'm in a crumpled heap with a line of dirt as my horizon and four horse hooves as moons setting into an ocean of fine gravel and dust.

It's a cold, clear night in January and I'm standing behind the tattered movie screen in one of California's oldest theaters watching bookend images as they move in reverse: bookends because the scenes are from the first breath of one of my deepest relationships all the way through to its last exhale, and in reverse because I'm watching from behind the screen, which makes the images run backward.

I silently rewind other memories like movie reels in my mind, scenes from my early struggles of chasing a dream all the way to the personal and creative rebirth that is this evening. But I know I'm only doing this to keep from crying at what will be on the screen any moment now.

There it is. I see my head bowed down, kissing a black Labrador's graying face on the day she died while I hold a picture of myself and her as a puppy. I see us swimming in a backyard pool on the same day, my hand on the scruff of her neck as I float next to her and guide her toward her last labored trip up the pool stairs. Where others have had life partners beside them during their empty moments, I had this dog, and her passing has left a space yet to be filled.

The air sort of staggers through my throat when I hear my own voice over the theater's sound system reading a letter I wrote to her that day she died, set like a soundtrack against the moving pictures. I look down at my hands to again hold off the tears because I know where my next steps lead. When the sound of my voice stops I walk out in front of the screen with my guitar.

I play the song I wrote about her to a theater full of people who have just watched our close-knit group of musicians play the twelve songs we wrote about four other letters, all from women who are seeing beauty rise from the wreckage of their own tragedies. But this song is called "The Table" and it is about my best friend, and both the letter and song were written more for the sender.

As the last chord rings out the other musicians join me to sing "Stand By Me," then one by one we walk off the wooden stage worn thin by the countless steps before us. We leave the songs and stories there in the fabric of the rugs scattered over the more splintered stretches of wood and I wonder if that's where they will stay.

This seems to be the end of a beautiful chapter of writing and performing songs about letters and we aren't yet ready to turn the page, so the next month we play another show at a local coffee shop to keep the feeling alive. It's a smaller room than the theater and the front door is open to the sounds of fire engines and buses passing by so the heat coming off the crowd can escape. I recognize many people in the first few rows from the theater show and think maybe they're here because they want to keep the feeling alive too.

One of those people is a young woman with long, dark hair seated down to my left, sometimes crying and sometimes shining as we play and tell the stories behind the songs. After the show she approaches me with a package, which she says contains some home videos and two letters written from her father to his best friend. I hurriedly shove the package into the cushions of the couch onstage, telling her that the furniture we're using as a set is really from my own living room and I'll take a look at everything when I get home.

∪

The home phone rings as I'm sitting at the kitchen counter with my mom and dad, talking about how I've spent the last couple of years immersed in this project with songs about letters, but I don't know what to do next. My mom picks up the handset and talks into the receiver and listens and hangs up the phone. She stands still for a moment, staring a few feet in front of her at a new hole in the pine flooring that only she can see and then says *Jane died.*

I've heard stories about Jane, a beautiful soul with a door always open to my mom and dad when they were just beginning their life together over a half century ago. And now my parents are 50 years older with that life of kids and grandkids and careers, these seeds sown in careful soil, grown and almost behind them and they are still here but Jane is gone.

My mom shuffles in her slippers over to the window above the sink and stares outside facing away from me and my dad walks slowly across the kitchen and wraps his arms around her. I watch their bodies rise and fall with halted breath as they cry together, they cry for Jane, they cry for their youth and innocence, they cry in quiet remembrance staring out the window until they are only one and I am only a witness.

A few weeks later I find the package from the woman in the cushions of my couch and pull from the envelope three letters and a few home videos. I watch one of the videos and as I stare at the screen I see myself. There I am on a surfboard, there I am smiling in the sun, there I am everywhere in this young man's energy and being. And there I am moving from feats of strength on a huge wave to feats of dependence in a wheelchair as my body succumbs to some sort of degenerative disease through the frames of the grainy home video. He is me, in the shape of our face and the shape of our lives, except that he is no longer here and I am, I am here watching the one thing that does not change in him, a smile big and beautiful all the way to the end.

I open the pages included with the home videos and find several lined, yellow handwritten pieces of paper, the first of which is addressed to me.

*   *   *

Alex,

First let me say that what you are doing with your For the Sender project is such an incredible thing. Not only is it beautiful and amazing, but it is necessary. So many people out there need the random acts of love that others give.

My daughter Tonya and I so enjoyed your show and are so grateful to all of you involved with your project.

I am including two letters that I wrote to my very best and dearest friend who was afflicted with and died of ALS, a disease know better as Lou Gehrig's disease. His passing after a long and agonizing battle is not why his story is so important, but how he handled his tragedy and found a way to turn it into an opportunity to give to and love others, that is the story.

His name is Frank Texeira, a Southern Cal surfer who lived loving others and figured out how to continue to love others long after his death. He did this through what he called "Big Fat Love." Explaining it all in this letter would prove impossible. Let me just say the very definition of Big Fat Love is exactly what you are doing with the For the Sender project.

I loved him so much as my own brother and we both agreed on and lived out our lives trying to give and be kind to others. I know his story and idea of Big Fat Love will inspire you. I only ask that you return the letters to me at some point in the future as they are the originals.

Thanks again for all you are doing. Somewhere I know my buddy Frank is smiling at your unique idea and way of sharing your gift of song in love for others.

With much Big Fat Love,

Dan

I begin to read the first letter from Dan to Frank and when I get to the word *God* I get a little uneasy because I have my own questions about God, questions for God, questions that still linger in the songs and letters from the performances we're doing now about the good that can come from seemingly senseless tragedy. Questions I know aren't only my own.

Frank,

Well my amazing friend, you have finally been set free from the suffering of this life. We, your family and friends, are here still, contemplating the events of the last five years, trying to sort out our feelings. My heart aches for more time with you and yet it soars over the waves just as you did on your board so many times. It soars because I know you are happy and right where you belong. If there is one thing that I learned for certain through all this, it is that God has, and will reveal purpose in all he does, even in and through great suffering. Your faith in this has given me wings, my friend.

You were the first surfer I had known. I am not a surfer, though you have left me wishing I was. They seem to be so in touch with the rhythms of nature around them. They approach things with the same extraordinary passion that they have for the sea and the waves. It seems to speak to them at a spiritual level. The same passion with which you lived your life.

I thank you my good friend for giving me so many wonderful and amazing gifts in our seven years together and in such a difficult time. As I watched Lou Gehrig's disease year after year try to take away your passion for life, I watched you fight back with love, grace, and kindness to all those blessed enough to know you, even when all you could do was smile and wink. You literally showed us how to live, and then showed us how to die while maintaining such character and integrity. You even created "BIG FAT LOVE." so that others could learn how to love as you do and pass it on. You are an amazing soul and not a day goes by that I don't ask myself, "Am I making Frank proud?" You see, you are still helping me to be better.

Some of the greatest gifts of all are all the amazing friends you have given me who I never would have known. These surfers and friends from your youth are now all that I have left of you, but they are such an amazing and wonderful part that you have now given to me. I have learned in all of this that God allows us to love in so many ways. I would never have imagined I could love a friend so deeply, so powerfully. We saw eye to eye on everything. It is as though we are "twin souls"!

And so, Frank, I can no longer look at the ocean without my heart aching for your presence, the magic in your laughter, the sound of your voice, and that twinkle in your eye as you smile at everyone you see. But then I realize you are not so far away as I may have thought, as the aching in my heart is gently massaged away by the sound of the waves, speaking to me now as they never have before.

I love you so much my good friend! Wherever you are, I know it is with God just as you told me you would be. I know you are on that perfect wave, in the tube on the left-hand break, just like you did here for so many years.

You have taught, and continue to teach, me so much. I can hardly wait for you to teach me how to surf when I get there!

With BIG FAT LOVE,
Your best friend and twin soul,
Dan

I read again the sentence about how Frank has shown the world how to live and then how to die. What a gift, to learn how to die. There's loss and struggle and longing in Dan's words and the letter leaves me with an image of him standing with a shovel next to an open grave, the fresh pile of dirt waiting to be returned to the hole in the earth. But he's not yet ready to bury his best friend.

I turn to the next letter, dated six months later, and something has changed. Something and everything.

Frank,

I will never forget the time we knew we were "twin souls." We saw the sun set at Lake Cuyamaca and you said, "The end of another great day!" I replied, "I think the sunset is just the beginning of the next sunrise!" You turned and looked at me with those piercing blue eyes and huge intense smile and said, "THAT'S AWE-SOME!" That was when we both knew this would be no ordinary friendship.

The sun is well below the horizon formed by the blue-gray mountains of the northern Sierra Nevadas, which seem faded tonight. Their majesty is upstaged by the tapestry of color, which seems more brilliant this evening than ever before. As I sit atop my favorite rock on the shore of Eagle Lake, I marvel at this display both above and below the horizon as the colors in the sky and on the water merge into one.

I look to my right at the boulders that form the shoreline of this magnificent lake, gazing at your favorite spot and wishing you were here looking at this sunset with me as we have so many times. We always had that in common, you and me, our appreciation of nature's wonders. I am not sad this time, however, and I must ponder why.

Is it because the wounds of your leaving are healing? Is it because this was always a place where we shared so much joy? Is it because I expected this when returning to such a place from our past? Probably all of these to one degree or another. Somewhere deeper, however, down past my everyday feelings and emotions, I believe it is something more. Something greater than all my wants, emotions, and feelings.

I believe it is something more spiritual. I think that just as every sunset is the promise of the coming day filled with hopes and dreams, yet undisclosed and unrealized, I also think the ending of our amazing and beautiful friendship here is simply the promise of realizations and discoveries about our friendship that I have not yet conceptualized. Any sorrow I anticipated feeling seems to have been replaced with the jubilant anticipation of what you will show me next.

Frank, my gratitude for all you gave me in friendship and all you continue to show me can never be reduced to words. Mostly it is the relationships you have paid forward to me. Your friends are now mine and I love them all: Dina, one of the most purely kind people I could hope to know. Scotty, such a loyal friend and a soul so much deeper than he is yet willing to show me. Then, Frank, there is your love, Michelle! You know, "the one in the red dress." In such a short time she has become a close friend that truly understands just how deep our friendship really was. We stumbled together through our loss of you, helping each other to remain standing through it all, and I will be forever indebted to her. Now she is a wonderful friend to my entire family.

These people have really shown that they are the true definition of BIG FAT LOVE and they are dedicated to your cause of spreading the word that we must give and do for our fellow man, expecting nothing in return other than the privilege of performing that act of love.

So now the sunset is but a whisper of pink and peach on a quickly darkening starlit sky. A sky so replete with stars that it seems there is not room for even one more. I smile as I remember the first time I shared this sky with you, so high in the mountains that we joked about being able to take them down one at a time and give them to those we love.

As our tongues grow weary, stomachs aching from laughter while telling "Frank" stories, Richard and I must make our way back to the truck in the dark over the same rocks and boulders that we had to carry you over on our last trip here together. Your disease prevented you from doing it yourself. I marvel at how you smiled

*and laughed while being carried down to your favorite
spot by the lake, not once showing disappointment or
bitterness. But then that was what you always did. As
I arrive at the truck and look back into the darkness toward the faint sound of waves on the rocks, I smile and
know that I will be back. What a fitting pilgrimage it is
to make in honor of my best buddy in the world and my
eternal fishing partner.*

*Frank, can you feel it? Can you smell it? As the eve-
ning breeze begins to swirl, it mixes with the smell of
juniper and pines and it is so refreshing.*

*Yes sir my good friend, the winds they are a
changin', and so is my heart. I AM REFRESHED! I
AM RENEWED!*

I love ya buddy!
BIG FAT LOVE my friend,
Dan

*   *   *

Light, gratitude, rebirth. An unburdened heart. And
not one mention of God.

The pile of dirt has been returned to the earth and
from it grow new friendships and awareness and Dan sees
Frank everywhere now, in the trees, the sunset, as if he
never left, only changed shape from skin to sky.

This letter is more a celebration than a memoriam.
It doesn't use God to explain anything away but has an

energy of redemption and renewal and love that feels more like God, with no sign of the word *God*. And it talks about love as an action, embodied in this Big Fat Love idea, which I know nothing about except that it seems to be about doing love instead of feeling love and I like that idea.

I sit looking down at the lined yellow pieces of paper in my lap and realize that writing a song about these letters would be as simple as picking up the guitar resting next to me on the couch. I can see parallels between Dan's letters and those from Emily, the woman who sent the letters that inspired the *For the Sender* project. There are two letters from Emily and two letters from Dan, both about best friends who have passed away, both written from a beautiful voice working through loss. And the video of Frank gives me a broader picture and a deep connection because I can see myself in him, I can watch his story unfold, I can write a soundtrack to it.

Outside the front window a jet races across the endless spring sky, white streaks cutting behind the frayed electrical wires scratched deep and unmoving against the blue. I too have what seems an endless sky to fly across, if only to cover the ocean of costs to put these songs about letters out into the world. I've lost track of the seen and unseen tolls of production and process and patience involved in making a little book with songs about letters, a little book I've sunk my time and resources into, only to print a few hundred copies to give away to family and friends and the letter senders and whoever else might want one.

This labor of love has unearthed something in the rich dirt of my dreams that loves to write. I cautiously hope this could become my living but I don't see the way forward, so I keep it buried and secret and quiet and some nights I still lay awake with my what-ifs sitting on the bed next to me, the loudest whispering *What if this is all there is, this small book of songs no one will read?*

But I know what it means to chase a dream as a singer-songwriter, for years asking these same kind of questions, and I will not let myself chase the same kind of dream as an author. So I've been thinking about find-ing other ways to make a living while we continue to play these small shows where we present the songs about let-ters. Maybe these performances are more of a reward to me than a step in a certain direction, a reward for time and patience and frustration and energy and expense, all costs I would be happy to pay again once I build up a re-serve of money and enthusiasm.

But that time is not now, so I put the letters back in their envelopes and slip a rubber band around the pa-pers and home videos. I'll give the package back to the woman, tell her thank you for sharing with me and to thank her dad too and I will move on, because there are things I must do to make a life and a living other than write books and songs about letters.

U

The horse is still standing there, a tempest gone quiet in the fading early summer light. Her ears are turned forward in question as she looks at me lying in the dirt and we're both unsure as to what has just happened or what to do next. I stiffly pull myself up and limp over to her and in her own sort of confusion she lets me pull the tangle of saddle and leather and metal off her body and put a halter on her and together we make our way back to her paddock, where I take the halter off and hang it over the aluminum-pipe rail.

I wrap the gate chain around the rusting metal post and drive myself to the hospital, where the doctor tells me *You better stay off that horse for a while, son* because I've ruptured multiple discs in my back which will require bed rest to heal and muscle relaxants to sleep.

I'm not sure what to do with the horse and it won't be long before I'm again lying in the dirt after another fall, but this time I'll find something buried there in the dust and blood. Something broken. Something that every relationship worth anything is built around, something that holds us together and anchors us to accountability and authenticity. And something which once broken must be repaired one small moment at a time, if ever to be repaired at all.

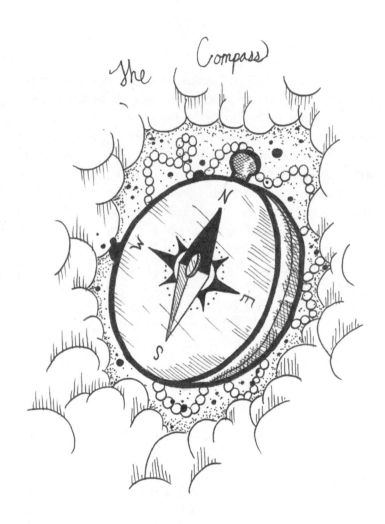

THE COMPASS

Your soul is like a compass;
tells you where to go,
but not how to get there.

— ARCHIE BUNKER

road to the barn

U

I lay in bed letting my body heal after the fall and read books about what humans think they know about horses and it's as if I'm reading about another kind of animal altogether, because the horses in the books are docile and respectful and want to be ridden and are good learners. The people in the pictures have sanitized magazine-ad smiles as they happily do their perfect drills in their clean shirts with their willing horses. I don't really see myself in the pictures and I definitely don't see the horse, so I abandon the books to a never-to-be-visited-again corner of my bookshelf and once I'm able to walk without leaning to one side I pile myself into my truck and make my way out to the barn through the choking midday traffic congestion.

I open the stall gate and the horse pins her ears back flat against the upper outcropping of her mane and walks away toward the far corner of her paddock, swinging her hindquarters around as I approach so her right rear leg is ready to kick. There's a drop in my stomach and it's not my pride that has fallen but something harder, something more elemental and physical because I can feel the power she has at her disposal and I know she's threatening to use it against me.

I get close enough to see something that I somehow haven't noticed before and my stomach drops even farther. *How did I miss this? How?* Her skin is rubbed raw in red and gray and black dime-sized spots, all in various stages of crusting over, behind her front legs where the cinch wraps under her belly and holds the saddle on her back. It's almost too painful to look at and I know these wounds are from someone else repeatedly tightening the strap under her belly until it cut into her skin and then making her work.

Some emotional and behavioral scars have already begun to show in her pinned-back ears and the busted discs in my back but this is the first and only physical sign I'll ever see pointing to some kind of past abuse, these scabs covering wounds so raw and deep that they'll eventually turn the hair that grows back white as a reminder of how worthless some humans can be.

After a few minutes of approach and retreat I slowly back away across the paddock and leave her facing the intersection of the two fences, her head thrust into the corner where she tries to escape the awful possibility of a person wanting to share the same space with her. I walk slowly at a limp back to the parking lot and as my truck crests the hill above the barn I can see the horse still standing there, like a child with defiant tears staring fiercely at the space where the walls of her room collide.

Except this is no child, this is a thousand-pound animal finding strength and solace in her belief that she can, she may, she will defend the last vestige of honor she has left after the wild has been destroyed and in its place remains only this human construct of fences and dirt lots and all these things that we have done.

U

I take this highway back and forth between the boarding facility and where I live because I can't keep the horse in my backyard with the fake grass and concrete and houses stacked upon one another. The drive leads me out through the city and eventually away from the burgeoning, bleeding mass of humanity that is Southern California and shows me what the landscape may have looked like centuries ago, before there were cell-phone towers on top of buildings on top of land cut deep by machines. Sometimes I wish I was there and not here, sometimes I wish I could find a place where humans still live more with the land than at its expense.

Enough time has passed for the moving images of Frank to fade from my everyday thoughts but even this highway can't take me away from the sameness I sense between us, no matter what I tell myself. My gaze shifts from the rugged hills to my rearview mirror, where I half expect to see Frank sitting there in the backseat, smiling back at me.

I turn my eyes back to the road just in time to see a freeway exit sign about a quarter-mile away that I haven't noticed before. It says *Lake Cuyamaca* and I search my memory for why I might recognize the name and I'm almost to the sign when I realize that this is the lake from Dan's letter, where they watched the day fade together and he called the sunset the start of another sunrise.

I slow down to take a picture of the sign because by now I know this isn't just an exit sign for a lake. This arrow painted on weather-beaten green metal is more like the needle on a compass showing me a direction to take but leaving the route a mystery. No map, only a compass, where instead of an *N* for North there's an *F* for Frank.

I speed up as I pass the sign and say out loud to myself *A compass but no map.* Now that the songs-about-letters project is over I'm trying to figure out what steps to take next, even though I still have no idea where I'm really going. So I've been looking at different kinds of maps, but not the kind I have here in the glove compartment of the truck. These different kinds of maps show streets to success and fulfillment that others have taken, printed in the dark, unyielding ink of history, boulevards paved with the stories of my heroes.

The exit for the horse barn is the next off-ramp and I pull off the freeway having a conversation with myself about how maybe it's not just me, maybe we all think we need these maps and our maps are books about how to train horses and make money and mend relationships and be *okay*. Our maps are television shows and sermons and newspaper articles, seminars and conferences and classes. These maps show one way to walk but there are other ways too, and no matter what they say these maps don't do the walking for us.

I take the right turn from the rural road into the barn thinking that maybe the more beautiful route, maybe my truer route, is one followed not with a map in hand but with a compass. A compass that guides the first step, then the next step, then the one after that, steps taken in the moment, over hills and creeks, through fields and deserts, under my own wild sky.

Thank you, Dan and Frank, for the compass.

Dan and Frank

∪

The only place besides the horse barn where I find some temporary refuge from the urban sprawl is here where the ocean meets the land. I'm on the beach early the next morning with Stella, watching her shuffle her paws in anticipation as she drops a tattered tennis ball in the shallows and waits for the circling water to carry it away so she can chase after it herself. She's an independent dog, more so than my old black Labrador Kona was. I sometimes still see that black Lab down here at daybreak, running slow and stiff, trying in her last days to keep up with the little brown explosion of puppy that was Stella.

As the next wave breaks I look through the spray drifting off the water and in a sudden flash of remember-whens I see myself with my neighborhood friends sitting out in the water on our surfboards, laughing and splashing in the mid-August sun. I look down and there we are lying in the warmth of the sand, talking about what to do for dinner and when I look back up the wave has crumbled and crawled up the sand and both images are gone. I can hear a Don Henley song about the boys of summer and Wayfarers and driving by your house even though you're not home and don't go back you can never go back here in the echoes of these crashing waves.

I watch Stella wade into the surf and think about how sometimes seconds and minutes and hours become an era, a golden collection of moments that moves slower in memory and defines its borders with a certain feeling of nostalgia or sentimentality or sadness or joy. These are the eras of childhood, first loves, and other new beginnings and before this morning I've only seen them in the rearview mirror, after they've come and gone.

But these memories on the beach tell me that I'm starting to see an era shift in front of me. My circle of friends has begun to scatter with the introduction of newborn babies, growing children, and touring and recording schedules, and we're rarely in the water or on the beach together anymore. I'm the only one without a spouse or child and I'm noticing a soft alienation creep in as I become the third or fifth or seventh wheel at our occasional family dinners, which once brought us closer together but are now becoming less and less frequent.

So over the past few days I've asked several people in this slowly diluting group of songwriting friends if they'd like to write a song about Dan's letters to Frank, with the hope that maybe new letters and songs will bring us back together again. Most of them don't have time because they are trying to stay afloat with their own responsibilities, and I understand. I know that new lives are being built and taking on new eras of their own, beautiful landscapes built on family and opportunity, but part of me wants to hold on to what used to be.

I've tried to hold on to eras before, even ones with fewer fond memories than those I've found here on the sand this morning. Like high school. I remember walking across my old high school campus long after graduation, talking to teachers and coaches, looking for a familiar hideaway from the real world in the hallways of my past, the very place where as a teenager I was still in the dirt, still germinating, not yet pushing up through the soil of my blood and upbringing.

Those who bloom early often seem to wither early and lately I've heard about second divorces and multiple stints at rehab for some of the cooler kids from high school. They were so popular then. But that was their era, not mine, and I wonder why I'd ever try to hold on to it. I suppose there's comfort in the familiar, even though everything that's now familiar once was new. I might as well embrace the new.

The sunlight creeps over the cliff and spills onto to the beach, which is the signal for Stella and me to leave before the sheriff drives by in his expensive off-road toy to start handing out $400 fines for having dogs on the beach. I doubt it was a dog who smoked those cigarette butts thrown in the rocks or let go of that balloon tangled in the seaweed, but the law is the law and rabid, dangerous, soul-stealing canines like this relentlessly joyful Labrador with a tennis ball in her mouth aren't allowed on the sand. This open space, this refuge may be free of buildings, but it's not really free.

So we traverse our way up the wooden stairs from the beach and by the time we get to the top and Stella shakes the salt water off her chocolate-brown coat, I have an idea. I dry her off with a beach towel threadbare from many mornings like this, push open my front door, and start searching for Jordan Pundik's phone number.

Jordan is part of the scattering circle of musicians with kids and he's moved to Nashville with his new family for an apprenticeship with a well-known tattoo artist. He also spends a lot of time on the road as the front man for the multiplatinum rock band New Found Glory and has a voice that has carried arenas full of teenagers through the push-and-pull uncertainty of growing up.

And for those reasons he's one of the only people I haven't talked to yet about Dan's letters. He's already gone across the country and I know he's busy with his kid and wife and touring. But if I'm going down this road of songs about letters again, I think someone else should be the singer, not me, and Jordan has the voice. Letting go of my own voice singing these songs I've written still feels right, a lesson in detachment born in the first collection of songs and letters where I sing on only a couple of tracks.

So my gut tells me to find his number, push the buttons on the phone, and wait. There are separations made by miles and there are separations made by choices, and they aren't the same thing. Sometimes the separations made by miles aren't nearly as wide.

Already in motion are wheels that will bring Jordan and his family back to my neighborhood, wheels in the shape of a newborn child for him and his wife, wheels that have taken him and other friends away but will bring this friend back.

But I don't know that yet, and neither does he. And when I ask if he wants to help write some songs about Dan's letters and be the singer in my new band, he says yes.

U

I'm saying goodbye to someone in a coffee shop and I don't really know her at all except for a few *hellos* here and there, but she hugs me and says a flippant *love you* in a been-there-done-that kind of way, only I haven't been there or done that with her and this doesn't count as love, this sharing of space and time and pastries. She hasn't carried me over rocks when I'm hurt or wrapped her arms around me in an empty moment or done anything at all besides sit next to me with a group of my friend's friends who have been talking about themselves a lot and preaching love as if it's a mindset or feeling or one of the hand-drawn winged hearts they post on their social-media pages.

I've eaten my blueberry muffin with building focus to steel myself against this talk about love and holding space and manifesting boyfriends and other neo-hippie chatter woven into every other sentence, traded like blankets between the talkers to keep themselves warm in their cold, harsh realities of underachievement and un-accountability. I kick myself under the table to remind myself not to be judgmental because this building of personal dramas and perceived importance is just a way of feeling significant, which everybody looks for. I know because I've done it too.

But I don't want to hear about how they can't quit coffee and Spirit is telling them they need to, or how they are becoming more aligned with their chakras since starting yoga at the new mother center. I don't want to hear about how they are manifesting a boyfriend or a career or a smoothie for themselves or how they are trying to hold space for me right now in the blissfully rare moments I do get a word in.

One of the talkers is a girl I know well, a girl old enough to be a woman but still a girl, who has learned to take but finds real giving and doing for others elusive. She's the best talker about love at the table and as we get up to leave and the *love yous* are thrown around like the napkins crumpled and tossed next to our plates, I watch her check her phone and make her way out the coffee-shop door, in all of her love, leaving her bill unpaid on the table.

I head south on Pacific Coast Highway toward home and as the traffic slows to a stop I feel the inside of my windshield to see if the crack left by a construction truck's stray rock has gone all the way through. My view of the Prius in front of me now matches my fractured view of this way of living, this mess of people on top of people on top of concrete and steel and my mind turns to how the talk at the coffee shop is mostly about self-help but it seems to be more self-ish help. It could be the frustration with the traffic or my windshield talking but I want to say to everyone around that table that maybe they don't matter like they think they do and if they got out of their own way maybe they could do beautiful things for the world and in turn themselves.

But I don't turn the truck around and drive back to the coffee shop and say that to them, because I know my frustration with them is only a reflection in this glass.

And hopefully they'll find their own compasses before too long, buried somewhere in those blankets of winged-shaped hearts they weave so well.

We start our first song in my living room when Jordan comes back to San Diego on vacation. He plays air guitar to show me the rhythm he feels for the song while

I follow frantically along on my guitar trying to keep up with his flying hands and within an hour we have a framework in place. I find Dan's letters in my desk drawer and wrap the lyrics around them: the sunset, twin souls, the carrying of Frank over the rocks, the reliance on faith, the slight shade of his first letter's longing and struggle.

I call it "Breathe The Sky" because the song unfolds into Dan's realization that Frank is everywhere and there's no need to be longing for what's already here. He's breathing in all that was his best friend, the mountains, the trees, the sky, all that Frank is and was and will become.

*   *   *

breathe the sky

remember when we watched the sinking sun
we were twin souls young on fire and running free
along the razor edge horizon
remember when you smiled and turned to me

the beauty

oh lord i
never felt so alive
oh lord i
wish i could

breathe the sky

dark clouds circled low overhead
the last time i was sitting here with you
your smile was all i thought you had left
i wondered how i'd ever make it through

without you

oh lord i
never felt so alive
oh lord i
wish i could
breathe the sky

and now the sun is setting on the lake tonight
just the beginning to another morning light
feeling you're still real and here by my side
if i could i would carry you all night

i'll carry you over
i'll carry you tonight
i'll carry you over
i'll carry you home

oh lord i
never felt so alive

oh lord i
wish I could
breathe the sky

oh lord i
(and the sun is setting on the lake tonight)
never felt so alive
(just the beginning to another morning light)
oh lord i
(if i could I would carry you all night)
wish i could
breathe the sky

*　　*　　*

As Jordan sings *carry you all night* I close my eyes and see a man carrying another man and there's strength and power and intention in that act. A feeling can't lift a person over rocks, but two arms can. I hit the stop button and as Jordan takes off the headphones I remember watching my dad walk over to my mom in the kitchen and wrap his two arms around her and that too is love, love in the doing.

A couple of days later I see a comment posted on the Internet under one of the videos from the night of the January performance. The song is called "My Love Will Find You" and the comment is from someone in the audience that night and says *One of the best nights of my life shared with great friends and gifted musicians and singers.*

I watch the video and as Jordan sings the choruses in response to Molly Jenson's verses, I notice that the special moments come when they sing certain words together. There's a beauty to their voices together that's deeper than simple harmony, something that can't be manufactured, and I wonder if this band I'm putting together should have a female voice to balance out Jordan's power with grace. Molly has sung with us before but hasn't written any songs so I haven't thought to ask her if she wants to be involved yet. Maybe she does, maybe she wants to write and sing and walk with us wherever these first few steps lead.

The more I think about the idea the more I like it and I call her and ask if she wants to be in the new band too, and she says *Yes, yes, a thousand times yes.*

I'm staring at my computer screen and just before I start going through the endless "are you sure" steps to delete a social-media account I see a comment from a "friend" I don't know under someone else's pedestrian post that never would be shared if it wasn't so easy to do. These are frail connections, these thin spiderwebs we weave, unlikely to survive the strong gusts of the real world. Technology allows someone to be there without really being there and sometimes that's a beautiful thing but most of the time it's a poor substitute for the real thing. And I need more of the real thing.

Music is no different and this computer I'm sitting in front of has made it possible for the musicians involved with the last project to be at different places at different times and still play on the same song. I lean back in my chair and think about how records used to be made with everyone playing in the same room. There was something special about the way those albums sounded. Small mistakes were part of the landscape and I could hear breaths and piano pedals and fingers sliding around on the fret board. Things were allowed to be more human. More of the real thing.

Later that night my guitar player and bass player and I drive up to Los Angeles to see the premier of a music documentary about a recording studio. We watch Nikki Sixx and assorted rock royalty get out of their cars and don't think much about it until someone takes our collective breath away as she walks toward us on the red carpet, talking to reporters and posing for pictures along the way. We three stand with our mouths open. It's Stevie Nicks and we are teenagers again.

Fleetwood Mac's *Rumours* may be one of the best albums of all time and Stevie Nicks is the magical, mystical, beautiful presence that runs through the record like a desert ghost. She would become the voice of an era after making *Rumours* at the recording studio featured in the documentary, an era of '70s California and Laurel Canyon and sex and drugs and rock and roll and dreams, so many dreams.

My guitar player has saved us seats in the theater to watch the movie and after Stevie Nicks makes her way past us we find our coats draped over the three chairs he's randomly chosen. I sit down and look at the woman sitting an arm's length away and I think something's wrong, maybe I'm in a dream, maybe this isn't real, because sitting here with me is Stevie Nicks. Right here.

She talks to people around her before the movie starts, people she knows who are sitting farther away from her than I am because she is *right here*, and when the room darkens she puts on her glasses. She takes them off again when she starts crying at scenes that show her past as a mirror to her present, photos of her cleaning houses back then during the recording of *Rumours* and an interview with her now saying *I told them I would not be cleaning houses for long.* I think about leaning over at the end of the movie and saying something to her about how I'm glad she didn't end up cleaning houses for long.

But I don't.

I leave the theater and drive home. And I smile as I pull into my driveway, not only because I could never dream up a scenario in which I'd watch a movie with Stevie Nicks, but also because the movie reflects my thoughts earlier that day about not relying on recording and collaborating across telephone wires and Internet connections. The studio featured in the movie is the kind of place where music is created all at once, with the band members in the same room playing together through a legendary soundboard responsible for albums like Nirvana's *Nevermind*.

The drummer for that band has since exploded into the stratosphere of rock stardom and he buys the soundboard from the studio when it goes out of business. He's put the documentary together celebrating both the studio and the soundboard, but it's more about the people and that era of recording and how beautiful and human it is when people are in the same room with each other, talking with guitars or drums or just the sound of their own voices echoing off the walls and into each other.

And I'm smiling because that's want I want to do. That's a band.

So Jordan, Molly, myself, and the core group of musicians who have played with me for a long time start getting together in my living room to record as a group, not only because I want the feeling of being in a band again but also because maybe we'll get a glimpse of that magic that can happen when everyone is playing in the same space and breathing the same air. We bounce ideas off each other for a song I've already written called "Never Let You Go" and run through it a couple of times before I push the record button. And we see what happens.

Sometimes I write a song about a specific feeling or situation and later see the meaning running through other scenes too and "Never Let You Go" is one of those songs. I write it while standing at the top of my stairs with my guitar for a woman who has brought grace and beauty into my life but I don't know how to tell her what she means to me yet. I write it for her, and the recording I make that day of my scratchy voice singing along with my old road-beaten guitar will only ever be heard by her.

A few days later I'm reading Keith Richards's autobiography before bed and he says *There's never one thing a song's about* and before I fall asleep I see Dan carrying Frank over the rocks, not letting him go, and then I see my dad holding my mom in the kitchen, not letting her go, and I realize that to me this song may be about the woman, but it will be about other things to other people. And maybe these images of my mom and dad and Frank and Dan are like some sort of compass buried in my guitar, pointing the song in a certain direction, and as I drift away I think maybe Keith Richards is right, maybe every song is that way.

A man can't always find the words, and this man is Dan as he watches Frank slowly deteriorate while they talk about taking the stars down from the sky and giving them to the people they love. This man is Frank as he wraps his arms around his best friend to be lifted out of his steel and wire wheelchair and carried over the rocks. This man is my dad wrapping his arms around his best friend to face a hard and beautiful and sad moment together. And this man is watching his best friend, an old black Labrador, slip away and turning to wrap his arms around a beautiful, gentle woman who has made him a better man and that man, that man is me.

*   *   *

never let you go

i can sing about redemption
i can sing about the pain
of watching my best friend
slip away into the soft summer ruin

but i can't sing a love song
so i want you to know
when i wrap my arms around you tonight

i may never let you go

FOR THE SENDER: LOVE IS (NOT A FEELING)

i may never let you go
i may never let you go
i may never let you go

because you make me a better man
you make me stand tall
higher than this steel and wire
like it don't matter at all

but i don't know how to tell you
what i want you to know
so when i wrap my arms around you tonight

i may never let you go
i may never let you go
i may never let you go
i may never let you go

so let the sun sink low
and the stars cover the sky
we can take one down
for you and i

maybe then i can show you
what i want you to know
when i wrap my arms around you tonight

i may never let you go (so hold me tonight)

i may never let you go (we'll float over streetlights)
i may never let you go (as stars grow older)
i may never let you go

i may never let you go (hope won't be over)
i may never let you go (if you hold me closer)
i may never let you go (as stars grow older)
i may never let you go
i may never let you go

*   *   *

My grandma has been in slow decline for more than twenty years and when she can no longer say her name my mom and aunt move her into a residential home with five other dying women. The years of twenty-four-hour care in her house as we wait for her to die have taken their toll on my family and this will cost less emotionally and financially, but it isn't easy to make the change and the only way to move her is to wait until we think she doesn't know any better.

My sister and I visit her for the first time at the new place and we don't recognize her because her hair is shooting out in every direction instead of being piled into a neat bun on top of her head. She's sitting upright on a couch, which we haven't seen her do in a long time, since no one has helped her get out of bed like this in years. The twenty-four-hour care people may have fixed her hair in the mornings, but other than that they were too busy doing crossword puzzles and checking their phones at the kitchen table.

But every day here they lift her out of bed and put her in a shower chair and bathe her and dress her and carry her to the couch and make her food and wipe her mouth when she spills and I think this is real love they're giving my grandma. She wouldn't eat much at her old house and had to be almost force-fed Ensure shakes. But here she has an appetite and she's started feeding herself with her plate on her lap and napkin tucked into her collar and I can't believe how she's shoveling the food into her mouth. It's like her body is being restored by the physical care given to her instead of disintegrating in the passive non-care she got before.

Her mind is still gone though, lost somewhere between where she's going and where she's been, and she doesn't recognize my sister or me as we make our way past the two dogs that belong to the owner of the facility and sit down beside her. She has spaghetti sauce all over her face and I can tell my sister is trying not to cry as she rubs the tiny old feet of the woman who used to be our Grandma, the woman who now stares blankly outside, acknowledging what we say with an occasional grunt that could just as well be heartburn.

Until the wink.

I'm staring at her drooping eyelids when I notice that the pale eyes underneath are focused on me before suddenly shifting into momentary brightness. Her left eye closes and opens again and she smiles and then an instant later she's back to staring blankly out the window.

The wink is weightless but it's like a bullet heavier than lead that hits me deep and reminds me of when my dog died with her head on my lap. Just as she passed away a single tear fell down her nose and onto my shorts and they told me at the time that it was only my dog's body reacting to death. I thought maybe otherwise at the time, but this wink, this wink is definitely no accident.

She is there.

I'll come back to see my grandma more often as the weeks pass and she'll surprise me by saying things in what used to be empty spaces like *Suffer day and night* and *I love you*. She'll reach up to touch my face and reach down to grab my hand and she'll be there in those moments. Every time I go to her she'll seem to become more aware and I'll be stunned one day when she'll struggle to say something and her face will change as she turns her head from the wall and she'll look into my eyes and say *I just can't talk*.

Soon I'll ask her if she wants to go outside and she'll nod ever so slightly, so we'll strap her into a small wheelchair and push her outside for the first time in a long, long time. We'll go across the street to the lake in the park and look at the ducks and she'll take a piece of bread and push it at them. I'll roll some bread into a ball and say *Throw it like a baseball, Grandma* and she will, she'll throw it overhand from her wheelchair all the way into the lake.

This is how I'll discover that she knows more than she's able to tell me and that she can hear what I'm saying and understand me.

By then I'll have spent years thinking she didn't know what I was saying to her, years I pictured her crawling up the staircase from a barely lit basement, toward a brighter light shining from under a door that always stayed just out of her reach. A door of deliverance, hiding a beautiful white light of escape and knowing. And a light that until now I thought she must only dream of while she fumbles in the flicker of the dim bulb hanging from the wet, dripping ceiling of this forgotten basement at the bottom of the stairs.

I'll find that this dim bulb burns bright.

But that will be then and this is now, this is only the beginning of the power coming back on, and it's time to leave so I lean over to kiss my grandma's forehead, I tell her thank you for the wink, that it's okay for her to go, that we'll miss her but be okay here without her if she wants to go. Three times I tell her.

And we leave.

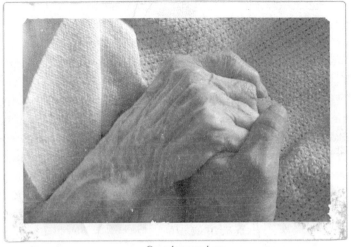

my Grandma and me

I remember Jack Tempchin on the night of our first show in the theater, asking when the next one is, so I know he wants to keep writing these songs about letters. I invite him over to check out Dan's letters and when he arrives he seems sort of quiet as we talk about a friend of his who's suffering through an illness, which I think may be the reason. We talk about my grandma who's still suffering and I say I've just said goodbye to her if she wants to go and Jack says *Well, maybe there's no goodbye.* We sit on the couch and I hand him Dan's letters and he starts to read.

He puts the letters down on the couch when he finishes and picks up his guitar and we start going back and forth with words and chords. Within an hour we write "There's No Goodbye" about Dan seeing Frank in his memories and everywhere around him and how maybe there really is no goodbye, maybe we just move from form to form and place to place. People say they know where we go and what happens to us, our soul, when we die but no one really does, and as we sing together I think about my grandma and the wink. I wonder where she goes, if she ever goes anywhere at all.

We record a demo of the song and as we listen back Jack gets up and walks to the window cut into the studio door and looks through it out to the ocean and I think that he's somewhere else right now, some kind of moment of reassessment. He's written a song called "Peaceful Easy Feeling" along with many other hits that have given rise to countless sold-out performances and record sales and big houses for one of the biggest bands ever and set the soundtrack for first kisses and first dances at weddings and funerals and it's all right there, standing at my door looking at the ocean.

But he is somewhere deeper than that and I can't quite place it, so I turn back to the studio speakers and listen with my eyes closed until the song ends.

U

Everyone is in the room, all six of us again. We have two microphones set up in the middle of our circle of chairs and we play and sing and record "There's No Goodbye" together to again see if we can capture the energy between us. We feel our way through the song and whatever mistakes happen we let happen. After the third take we think we have it so we listen back, and from now on this is what we will do as much as we can. We will record these songs together and we will let mistakes be mistakes because we can hear that maybe there's something to this, maybe there's something different we can hear living there in the space between us.

*   *   *

there's no goodbye

there's no goodbye
there's no farewell
that's the way it's meant to be
far as i can tell
though we may never meet again
there's no end to our road as friends

and the things we did together
gonna make us live forever
you and i
there's no farewell
there's no goodbye

there's no goodbye
things just move on
and the sunset's just the start
of tomorrow's dawn
we sat and watched the stars come out
talked and wondered what this life is all about

and the things we did together
gonna make us live forever
you and i
there's no farewell
there's no goodbye

we carry each other
from day to day
life gives us so much
love and beauty
then takes it all away

there's no goodbye
there's no farewell
that's the way it's meant to be

far as i can tell
though we may never meet again
there's no end to our road as friends

because the things we did together
gonna make us live forever
you and i
there's no farewell
for you and i
there's no farewell
there's no goodbye

*   *   *

I come back to the horse the day after she pins her ears and the next week and into the next month and if I move slowly sometimes she allows me within arm's length. I take those moments with silent gratitude and put salve on her belly wounds to help them heal and keep the flies out and I trace my fingers along her chiseled contours and up through her mane, but mostly I tell her about my day and what dreams come to me in quiet moments. She begins to know what I feel like and what I sound like and those times of small trust when she lets me come closer become more frequent, even though I can tell that it's much easier for her to run away than to trust. Every time I leave her I wonder what else happened in her past to cause her this kind of worry and fear.

One day she lets me wrap my arms around her neck and as I count the seconds before I feel her tense up I wonder if maybe time doesn't exist for her. Maybe she isn't comparing how long she stood calmly with me yesterday to how long she is standing calmly today and I shouldn't expect her to behave a certain way within a certain period of time. Maybe to her there's no measurement, no metric, no quantifying of experience based on seconds or minutes or hours or days or weeks or months or years. There's only the now and now she's letting me touch her neck. But that's only for now and I should be here for it.

So I look at my fingers through the mane that runs in layers across her neck and the strands seem so detailed that I can pick them out one by one. And it's as if I've never really looked at my hands before, I feel like I can crawl into the calluses. I'm sinking into the moment and there's some kind of refuge and expansion here, some different kind of presence, and I think that maybe this is what people try to find when they do their yoga in hot rooms.

At the same time I can feel the lingering pain of the busted discs in my back and I know that the horse won't honor impatience or expectation or what has been or what will be. I must leave my grand plans and maps outside the gate when I enter her stall and bury my means of measurement when I close the gate behind us. I can only bring some kind of instinctual internal compass to lend direction if we begin to take steps.

Because I only have the moment with her, and to allow each one to unfold on its own will soon reveal beauty I couldn't have imagined and reinforce my thought that perhaps our definition of time is irrelevant, without meaning or purpose except to serve as a cupped hand in which we must all tend our flames.

The Flame

THE FLAME

Poca favilla gran fiamma seconda.

— DANTE, *Paradiso*

Jesse Lewis

⌣

There's a flame spreading under my skin as I sit lightly in the saddle on the horse's back for the first time since the fall. I imagine the fire burning away everything I don't need, all this fear and uncertainty, and the horse stands calmly for a few minutes until I ease back down one foot at a time into the same dirt in which I fell and this is a first step, maybe we are getting somewhere.

The next morning I take her out on the short trail system running behind the barn because I think she may be calmer outside the arena and away from the chaos of cars coming and going. I climb onto her and silently pray that she doesn't take off running and as we leave the barn I tell her *It's okay* and tell myself that this is a leap of faith we must take to keep moving toward somewhere better than where we've been.

She doesn't take off running but she spins and stomps and gets more and more worried and agitated as we get farther from the barn and I don't want to push it so after a few minutes we turn around and head back. These may be small steps but they're steps in a better direction, the allowing to be brushed and handled and saddled and somewhat ridden, and I take these steps as little victories. Next time we won't ride alone and maybe that will give both of us more confidence.

So a few days later I take the horse farther out behind the barn with a lady who says she knows a good trail. We follow her and her horse away from the relative sanctuary of paddocks and round pens, across a field and toward a busy road with a dirt path running alongside it. They take a random turn in between two houses to get to "another trail" and we follow them and keep following for a while according to her weakening reassurances of *I think it's this way.*

We eventually get lost and end up on hot pavement in a residential neighborhood with cars racing by and honking and neighbors peeking out from windows at the huge animals they usually don't see on their street. No one we ask knows how to get back to the barn, they don't even know it exists. Daylight is fading and I'm surprised the horse hasn't yet crumbled with worry into her past and as I sit in the saddle with my head almost hitting a street sign I think to myself that this in itself is a victory.

And it's me who's beginning to crumble with shaking frustration at the lady who has gotten us lost when my horse pulls in another direction and something tells me to trust her, so I let her take her own steps across someone's lawn at the corner of two random streets. She turns down one of them and toward other streets and between houses and I let her go and within half an hour she has us within sight of the barn. The same pull toward the familiar that has agitated her and made her stomp and snort in protest a few days before is bringing us home.

We ride through the barn gate and someone asks *Where the hell have you all been?* and I well up with an emotion I don't recognize but it's something like trust and pride and relief, something I carry with me the rest of the night and into the next day.

We are getting somewhere.

U

The few hundred copies of the book given to the audience in the theater that January night have begun to exchange hands and it's still the noncommittal middle ground that Southern California calls winter when I find myself sitting in the office of a man in charge of a publishing company. He offers to release the book and two more yet to be written and invites me to talk about the letters and sing the songs at a series of events in different cities to support the book.

I don't have a literary agent or an editor or whatever else people have when they sign a publishing deal but this all sounds like a good idea to me and before long I'm in a chair in the sky on the way to New York for one of these events. When I get there I talk and sing for a quiet theater full of people and I'm grateful they listen at all because my memories of playing songs in bars as background music for dramas in dark corners are still etched deep.

I listen to the other speakers at the event and they all have their own message and story and one man onstage speaks in a voice from somewhere in my past. When I listen to him and close my eyes I see a younger self looking for some sort of hand to help me up out of the shallow hole I'd fallen into and judging from the strength of his audience I know I'm not alone.

He talks about his life and the lessons he's still learning from great teachers who are dead but still teaching before bringing onstage a mother who has just lost her son in a tragic mass shooting at an elementary school. I struggle to hold myself together as she talks about how her son Jesse made the ultimate sacrifice to shine a light on a deficit in this world and her story is so beautiful that I hardly have time to start breathing normally again before she is already off the stage. I see her backstage afterward and tell her I want to give her one of my books with letters and songs about beauty rising from tragedy as a thank you for sharing her own story. But by the time I find one sitting on a table in the lobby of the theater and bring it back to her, she is gone.

I turn to the wall of glass fronting the street and make my way toward the building's exit and see a hurried woman grasping for her handbag and coat and umbrella as she struggles to push her way through one of the doors. I manage to get there in time to hold it open for her and as she passes by with a small smile I see my heart exploding into her. Not the blood of my body but the whole of whatever good in me washes over her and in an instant the picture is gone. I let go of the door handle confused by the image of an exploding heart but I think the source is somewhere in the story I've just heard about the real blood of Jesse, the real exploding of a heart that has given life to others.

I head out of the building and turn down the block just in time to see a toddler stumbling toward a homeless woman, who is crumpled up against a wet, dirty wall in a mess of cardboard and cloth. The little girl is wearing a bright pink jacket and holding a single dollar bill in her tiny hand and as she approaches the broken-down woman she thrusts the clutched piece of paper in her direction. I don't see a parent anywhere around, all I see is this small child holding a dollar bill out to a street-stained woman who looks back at the child with an expression that is at once incredulous, stunned, and grateful.

I look away before the dollar bill passes from the clean hand to the dirty one because I want to keep that last image burned in my memory. I know I'll remember that photograph moment of the child and homeless woman for a long time, and it's not because the little girl is thinking or feeling or manifesting something for herself.

And sometimes even now as I pass by people leaving grocery stores or entering train stations or walking down the street I imagine my heart exploding into them with all the beauty and good I can give and I wonder if in some small way they can tell. And if maybe they are doing the same thing to me.

∪

Another lady at the barn has asked to ride the horse while I'm away, saying she knows all about this breed and will take good care of her. The horse probably won't be getting out of her stall much for a couple of weeks so I say okay.

The next week I hear from a friend who also has a horse at the barn. She tells me that the lady doesn't know as much as she claims and the horse is being run into the ground, deteriorating into a jumbled mess until she finally escapes from the barn late one afternoon and runs and runs and runs, away and down streets and toward the highway before she is corralled in an apartment-complex parking lot by a man who opens his door to block her between cars.

The lady is asked to leave the barn and not come back and I'll be home in a few days but the time can't pass fast enough. I drive straight from the airport to the barn and halter the horse and she seems okay until I reach for the saddle. She pins her ears and starts working herself into a lather and barely allows it on her back and when I lead her out into the arena she won't allow me to get on her at all. She spins and spins and spins when I try to put my foot in the stirrup and I spend almost an hour watching her escalate into a frenzy with no semblance to the horse that brought me home after being lost in the residential neighborhood.

I can feel the tide of frustration and fear and sadness and uncertainty rising in me and I ask her *Why are you doing this?* and *Weren't we getting somewhere?* and *Weren't we trusting each other?* and *What happened to you to make you like this?* but the horse just keeps spinning and rears twice before I run out of questions. Whatever happened between that lady and the horse seems to have unlocked a deep door in the animal that I can't find, no matter how many questions I ask.

An old cowboy saying flashes through my mind that says sitting on a horse is like sitting on a mirror. As I watch the horse chasing her own trail of dust around me, scattered and lost and frustrated in the middle of the arena, I can see myself scattered and lost and frustrated in the center of this circle of dirt.

The reins are wet in my hands with gritty sweat, almost granular with the dust. I wipe one hand on my jeans and think maybe this cowboy saying is a direction we could go, a compass needle pointing us out of this mess toward changing what's going on in me to change what's going on in the horse.

And maybe it's about changing my frustrated and confused questions of *Why do you have to be like this?* and *Weren't we getting somewhere?* to get answers other than these anxious spins and pinned-back ears.

I look down at the hand still holding the reins and the cowboy saying runs through my head again and I don't know how to change these questions and answers but I can try changing what's in front of me right now. And if we're a mirror to each other in the moment, then this is about her sensing my being and my sensing her being and neither of us being able to cover up the truth about what we are: scared, uncertain, and worried, all reflecting back on each other over and over again like the repeating mirrors in a carnival fun house.

My gut says changing the reflection could start with quieting the physical connection between us so I ease my grip on the reins and halfway close my eyes to keep from focusing my anxious attention on her. I take in the longest breath I can through my nose and watch the air leave and within a handful of exchanges most of what's left of my frustration has started to trickle out.

I can feel that the horse has already begun to slow her spinning and after a few more circles she stops and as I open my eyes she lowers her head and turns in toward me. I don't try to get on her, I only gently place my hand on the tangle of mane between her ears and say *Okay.* Her head lifts slightly and I catch my breath, because there it is.

The same look is there in her eyes, the look I remember from the day I got her, a small flickering flame of something beautiful asking to come out. This time it's there for a few moments longer than before, until a diesel engine loudly backfires outside the barn, sending the birds in the branches above our heads skyward.

And the small flickering flame retreats, far away from this manufactured cacophony, back to the open fields, the wild sky, the more beautiful time from which it came.

∪

I'm in a bar with a congressman and a producer on a rainy night in Atlanta, where we're all speaking at the same event. We're eating wings and watching the basketball playoffs on TV and talking about ways to get the congressman's message of mindfulness into communities when the producer pulls out his phone to show us a video.

He says that the footage is from a documentary he's doing and we watch on the small screen as a young boy gives money he's raised to kids in Rwanda for college. The boy has set up his own foundation whose message is to choose love and help others in the wake of the killing of his six-year-old brother, Jesse, who was gunned down in a mass shooting at Sandy Hook Elementary School in Connecticut.

And this brother's mom is Scarlett Lewis, who I've just seen speak at the event in New York. The producer tells me that he's friends with her and I tell him I wish I could have given her my book that day so she could see what we're doing, because maybe we could raise money for the foundation with some songs about her story. But he's already given her the book, she's already read it, and soon after Atlanta I'm handed my next compass. Two of them.

*   *   *

Dear Alex,

I enjoyed seeing you at the conference in February. That was only a short time after my 6-year-old son, Jesse, was killed in a mass shooting at Sandy Hook School. It's been almost 5 months now and I am still in shock. I miss him so much.

That December morning an angry young man shot through the glass doors of the elementary school and proceeded to gun down everyone in his path until he heard police sirens and shot and killed himself. He entered my son's first grade classroom and mercilessly continued his killing spree until his automatic weapon ran out of bullets. During this delay Jesse yelled to his friends, "Run! Run now!" Following the direction of

Jesse's clear thinking, nine of the children were able to run out of the school and were saved. When the man got his weapon working again he shot my son in the head . . . I have to imagine looking into his eyes. My brave little boy.

I heard there had been a shooting at my son's school but never in a million years thought my son would be affected. I raced to the school upon hearing the news and arrived just as the children were being released to their parents at the firehouse that sits directly in front of the school. I searched frantically, asking everyone if they had seen my son, even running up to the military soldiers strapped with grenades riding back from the school on an Army jeep, "Have you seen my son?"

We waited for hours, giving details of what Jesse was wearing and pictures. I had a long time to reflect and I knew if Jesse was taken from us that he had been brave and true to the end. After hours of agonizing waiting, the police confirmed our Jesse had been killed. I felt I had to be strong for Jesse's brother but I didn't know how I would go on. Through the wake, funeral, and ensuing weeks I was held up through an entire world's prayers, a national outpouring of sympathy, and the comfort of my family and friends.

I have seen unconditional love I never imagined. I have experienced generosity of spirit that far exceeds earthly expectations. I have witnessed forgiveness in hearts that can heal the world. I feel blessed and amazed by the miracles that have come out of this horrific trag-edy. All this goodness, yet the aching loss that remains in my heart is one that I will carry with me for the rest of my life. Still, the joy of knowing we lived fully and loved unconditionally is my saving grace.

I was asked if I would be interested in writing a let-ter to Jesse for you to turn into a song. I feel honored by this privilege. Jesse is a song to me, a beautiful melody that God gave me the music for and I helped to write the words here on Earth. It is a masterpiece that contin-ues to unfold even while he is in heaven. His is a song about grace, beauty, light, and love, always. Also about strength, courage, determination, and celebration. That is a decision.

Love Never Ends,
Scarlett

Attached to her note to me is a letter she's written to her son and a few photographs and at first I'm kind of thrown off because her voice seems more to be speaking to an adult rather than to a child. This isn't a letter to a six-year-old. But as I read I realize that Scarlett is talking to her son, and she's writing like this because she feels that he's in a place where he can understand her words and she doesn't need to talk to him like a six-year-old.

But the deeper reason may be that this letter, perhaps more than any other I've ever received, is written more for the sender.

My dearest, sweetest, most precious Jesse,

I write to you because my heart is broken open and the fresh red stains everything now. My yearning for you surpasses all reason for I know I will never touch you again here. I feel so low at times that my body could dissolve into the dirt and join you. I am at peace with this, but then something lifts me up, a bit. I search for you now in all things. And somehow I find you everywhere. You are my greatest teacher—and of all the most important lessons there are to learn . . . you have taught me that love never ends.

How do I start a letter for someone whom the longing of my heart is beyond words? My beloved child, to whom I gave birth and love and adore with all of my being . . . I want you. You are part of me, and I am a part of you . . . so we must be, still. I want you as the desert cries out to a gray cloud, heavy with moisture. I hold you as a plant's roots cling to the soil, determined for survival in their grasp. I need you as a rose opens its magnificence to the warm, nourishing sun. I sing to you as the robin chirps in anticipation of the sky-blue eggs she will lay in spring. I remember you as a horse rests under a tree in the dappled sunlight on a warm summer day. I love you as deep as the core of the earth and as high as where you are now. I love you, I love you, I love you. You love me back painted on the side of a rusty railroad bridge, "I Love U" in fresh white paint.

My human mind cannot grasp what has happened and why your little leg is not slung over mine as we slumber. You should be with me. You belong with me. I am your mama. I see you many times a day . . . running past me on your way but always our eyes meet and you say, "I love you Mama." If I close my eyes I can feel you . . . a cool hint of a breath on my cheek—or is it the brush of an angel's wing? I long to enfold you in my arms, to rock you in my gentle embrace, to offer you all that I have, and all that I am, again. But then I do, in my dreams you come to me in the flesh and I am able to hold you, to feel the pinchable skin, to squeeze those places I know better than my own.

I love you, I love you, I love you.

I love you scripted by a skywriter temporarily in the cloudless sky.

Before you left, I believed in God and heaven. Now I am blessed with a knowing . . . of where you are and perhaps even a glimpse of God's plan for you, and for us. I trust in God and knew before I lost you that He is the One that gives, and takes away. I understand my purpose now but am anguished that I must walk this path without you.

I love you, I love you, I love you.

I love you as you love me, and the world, with your beautiful soulful message of nurturing, healing love . . . full of wisdom enough to heal all of humanity.

I feel your presence within me. I feel you all around me. I understand now that you have been released and are not bound by the limitations and constraints of this earth. I know that time has no relevance where you are and that you can feel my love from all dimensions and it must bathe you in a continual warm light. I long for dreams where I can feel your skin, kiss your cheek, and run my hand over your body. During the day I talk to you, sometimes in the language we shared here and sometimes as how you are now . . . a powerful spirit who guides and directs so many here on Earth who only now understand the profoundness of your existence and your eternal energy.

I love you, I love you, I love you.

I love you like the message you scrolled in the frost on my car window the last time I saw you.

I long for the day when I can be with you. I feel blessed with the gifts you left for your brother and me, your loving messages that brought comfort and healing and will inspire many others. The blessed people you brought to my door . . . who held me when I was inconsolable . . . the love that exceeds all expectation. Your sacrifice brought attention to the world's deficit and I believe a shift has occurred because of your death and the many others who lost their lives alongside you. I will do my earthly best to turn this tragedy into love. Love never ends like how I love you.

I love you, I love you, I love you.

But for now I must be content to see you in the blue-bird that flashes his brilliance in my deepest moment of despair. Your presence is an act of kindness bestowed through love and compassion; a smile, or touch. An undiscovered picture of a rare moment with you filled with loving grace, a toy soldier found in an unexpected place. I think of where you are as the sun sets on God's canvas, and then rises again as a promise. A glimpse of you in my mind's eye and in silent prayers said in solitary midnight meditation.

I love you, I love you, I love you forever.
Your Mama

*   *   *

Jesse and Scarlett

I call her the day after I read her letters as I'm driving out to the horse and we talk about how she does miss the physical side of Jesse, what she could hold on to, but what she really loves about him is something that hasn't gone anywhere and can't be taken away. This reminds me of my high school physics teacher who, in between making David Letterman references I didn't understand in the middle of class, talked about some kind of law that says energy can never be destroyed, only transferred. I tell her maybe she loves who he is and was in the space in between the bone and the blood and the skin, whatever's in there that makes each of us an individual, maybe that's what she loves, and that never goes away. And she says *Yes, yes . . . the soul.*

She tells me about the photographs in her letters. She tells me about being out on the river in her kayak and looking up at the sky and saying *I love you, I love you, I love you* to him when an unusual wind blows her back under a bridge she's already passed and she looks up to see *I love U* painted on the rusting metal trellis. She tells me about getting out of bed to go to the bathroom one night and coming back to find one of his favorite toys next to her pillow where it hadn't been before. She tells me about seeing the words *I love you* written in the sky just as she'd been saying the same thing while looking toward the heavens, the same thing she says when she wants to be close to him. *I love you, I love you, I love you.*

I say maybe her internal radar is stronger now for seeing these things, these signs that are all around us but sometimes we don't recognize until some kind of tragedy hits, the same way Dan sees Frank everywhere around him now and knows that Frank hasn't really gone anywhere. We talk until I start to lose reception and as the signal fades she says goodbye and thank you and she hopes we can ride horses together the next time I'm on the East Coast.

I pull into the barn and remember a story I recently read about a little kid and a dog. The dog has just died and everyone is crying but the kid, who says he knows why dogs don't live as long as humans. The mom asks him why and the kid says because dogs learn to live the important lessons, like being good to each other and having fun, way before humans do. So the dog's life doesn't have to be as long.

Jesse's probably somewhere running around with that dog right now.

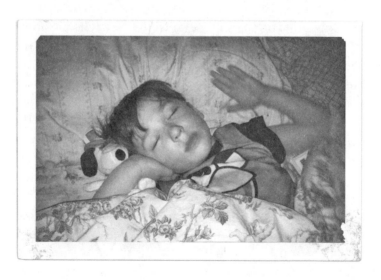

U

I'm downstairs at the piano thinking about the bullet that killed Jesse. Where it came from, how it got into the gun that got into in the hands of the mind that told the finger to pull the trigger. Lately every media source is flooded with talking heads screaming about gun control or lack thereof and the experts all think their way is the right way but I don't know what the right way is. Everyone has an answer but no one has an answer that everyone can agree on. Someone makes the bullets, someone sells the bullets, someone makes the gun, and someone sells the gun. But my gut says that maybe the most important someone is the one who pulls the trigger.

And in the end it is not a gun, not a man, not a law that tears apart Jesse's flesh, but a bullet that doesn't get to choose where it goes. I wonder what the bullet would say.

So I close my eyes and begin to play and I am the bullet.

*   *   *

bullet

they took me from the fire
metal forged my skin
for what darker of desires
lay in the hearts of men

then they put me in a box
with others just like me
high upon a shelf
for all the world to see

i could have landed in a twelve point
under amber autumn sky
or in the old fallen willow
where paper targets die
but i don't make those kind of choices
i have to go where i am sent
i never know where i am going
until i know where i went

he took the box down in secret
and left me in his room
underneath a glowing screen
where he drowned himself in doom

until he had enough one day
when he took me in his hand

and put me in a darker place
where i heard the hammer slam

i could have flown over the ocean
in an officer's salute
or taken down your killer
before he had time to shoot
but i don't make those kind of choices
i have to go where i am sent
i never know where i am going
until i know where i went

i flew
closer
and closer
i flew
closer
and closer
i flew
closer
and closer
and closer
to you

but i didn't mean to hurt you
i had to go where i was sent
i didn't know where i was going
but now i know where i went

*   *   *

I ask Molly to sing the song because I think her voice will be a compassionate contrast to how people usually think about a bullet, this lethal piece of lead that has no choice in where it's being sent. We record the song as a band together in the living room and I put Molly in the adjacent bathroom to sing so the noise from the drums doesn't bleed into her microphone.

I'm playing piano and can't see her since she's in the bathroom but I can hear her in my headphones as she shuffles the pieces of paper with the lyrics and says *Okay*. We haven't really rehearsed the song except for a few run-throughs to learn the melody so she isn't familiar with the words yet and is singing them off the pieces of paper. About halfway through the song I notice something different in her voice and by the time she sings the last line I can tell she's crying.

When I hear the change in her voice is when she realizes she's the bullet.

A light rain drifts down from the darkening sky outside as I sink into the couch, all kinds of drained from recording "Bullet." Mentally because I've spent the morning setting up the recording session and producing the song, emotionally because Molly's reaction is a mirror to my own that I've had to keep in check until now just to get through the session, and spiritually because the song carries a different weight than anything I've done before, a weight I've never had to carry.

A semi-lucid haze somewhere between being awake and asleep settles around me and I look out the window at the trails of water trickling down the glass. My mind starts to wander and I land on the thought that there's nothing I can do to stop the rain. I can't hold it back or change it or fix it, and if I could I'd be disrupting a cycle that has run for ages, a cycle of dark and light and storm and calm and all that is the very nature of life, the very reason we exist at all.

Water changes form but it doesn't try to change form. It just does. And no matter what form it takes, water doesn't resist its path or what carries it. The river is carried by the land, the cloud is carried by the wind, the raindrop is carried by the tension between the earth and sky, the same tension of gravity that holds me to the ground. And I know that I too am water, my blood and bone is water, and so I'm also part of the cycle of dark and light and storm and calm.

I'm shaken from my thoughts by movement outside the window, down below on the street, where I see a neighborhood woman running from the rain so her outfit doesn't get wet. I know her well enough to know that she also runs from the rain in her life with feel-good affirmations she posts on the Internet about how everything's always okay when those who know her also know everything's not okay and the world she affirms is not the world she lives in. It's not the world any of us live in.

She isn't the only one being told to run from the rain on life's edges to the umbrella of self-help books and pharmaceuticals, toward some sort of centerline in the dirt that is drier and so must be better than where she is now. But where she is now is the present moment, and if the present moment is rain, maybe something beautiful would happen if she let the rain fall there where she stands. Maybe it would wash away the dirt and grease caked on her spirit and leave her clean and strong, just as the steadily increasing drizzle is washing the dust from the leaves on the orchid tree standing outside my window.

I drift away again to the pounding rhythm on the roof and think about how some people carry a darkness that can't be glossed over or run away from and maybe that's because without the darkness in them there would be no light in others. I remember walking as a child through the German concentration camp at Dachau on Christmas Day and imagining myself freezing in the stark bunkhouses and being tortured and dying in a pile of other emaciated people and asking my dad *How could people do this to each other?*

Maybe some people have to carry this weight of our past transgressions on each other, a weight heavy with the eradication of entire cultures and human-inflicted brutalities. Because if energy can't be destroyed, only transferred, then someone must carry that weight so I don't have to, so I can in certain moments feel as if I never want to die because all of this around me is so beautiful.

Maybe the guy who killed Jesse was carrying that weight.

U

I'm invited to perform and speak at a seminar on happiness so I drive downtown to play my songs and tell my story. The coffee-shop talk about love and self-help is still on my mind and before long I say that we come to these seminars to be inspired because we like that feeling, so we keep coming, but being inspired isn't enough and we have to take the next step of actually doing something. Otherwise it's just selfish money spent to feel a certain way, to walk around talking about manifesting and whatnot, which is like buying a couple of whiskeys at the bar, drinking them down, and talking about how great we are.

As I talk I notice that I'm locked in one of those moments where I can't believe I'm saying this kind of thing at this moment in this setting, but I can't stop so I say that this idea that we have to help ourselves before we can help others is silly, because we don't have to be "okay" to buy a taco for a hungry person on the street. And maybe the compass needle for finding our path in life points toward taking a small step in service, maybe that's the first step toward being "okay." And again I think *Uh-oh, that's why these people are here, to be okay. To heal.*

But I say most of us don't need a healing anyway, we need a resurrection born in small things.

There's a small silence and then one person claps and then another and another until they all clap and stand up and I wonder if maybe I'm not the only one. Maybe other people are tired of feeling inspired and holding these maps of motivation but not taking any steps in any direction. And maybe other people think that love can be found in the doing, however small the action.

So I keep talking. There's just been a devastating tornado in Oklahoma and I say that we've all seen beauty rise from the wreckage before in other situations, some sort of flower pushing up from the ashes that soon becomes an entire field, but we often only get the front-page news when we hear about tragedy. We hardly ever hear about the good that may later come from it, because sometimes it takes a long time and we're not patient, the news media isn't patient, the Internet certainly isn't patient. But in time some kind of beauty comes on the heels of tragedy and maybe one needs the other, and hopefully we will hear about that happening in Oklahoma.

Afterward a woman takes my hand and says thank you and that maybe she just needs to be patient with the darkness and give real pieces of love when she's in the middle of it all instead of just thinking about it.

Because the darkness is there, for all of us, and all we can do is answer with some kind of spark. Like a taco.

I drive home from the seminar thinking about Scarlett's letter and how the song about the bullet can't be the only one, because her words are also about celebration and light and love. I think that there needs to be some sort of message from Scarlett to Jesse about the joy he brought her in life and still brings her every day. A song of celebration, which is a word I remember from her letter.

But by the time I pull into my driveway I'm seeing other pictures and different words are flooding through me and I push past Stella's big brown sleeping body at the back door and open drawers looking for the pen I never seem to be able to find when I need it most. The photos that Scarlett sent with her letter are flashing through my mind, images of the bridge, the sky, the chalkboard. And the frosted-over window. Jesse's reminders that he loves his mom are everywhere in those photos.

So I write a letter as a song from Jesse to his mom.

*   *   *

so you would know

i wrote it high up in the sky
white bright against the blue
then again across the bridge
where the wind would carry you
and in the frost on your window
just before i had to go

so you would know i didn't leave you
so you would know i won't forget you
so you would know
every lonesome road you roam
miles away from hope and home
remember to look where you may go
i wrote love there so you would know

we pray the lord our souls to keep
but my soul sings out loud
a forgotten melody
we must remember now
from dark skies to shining sea
where there is love there is me

so you would know i didn't leave you
so you would know i won't forget you
so you would know
every lonesome road you roam

miles away from hope and home
remember this where you may go
i wrote love there so you would know

to chase the dark into the light
come what may will come what might
remember this where you may go
i wrote love there so you would know

so you would know i didn't leave you
so you would know i won't forget you
so you would know
so you would know

every lonesome road you roam
miles away from hope and home
remember this where you may go
i wrote love there so you would know

to chase the dark into the light
come what may will come what might
remember this where you may go
i wrote love there so you would know

to never let a day slip by
without your face raised to the sky
remember this where you may go
i wrote love there so you would know

that there is only one way out
where we whispered we must shout
remember wherever you may go
love is forever and now you know

*   *   *

Later that night I'm standing by myself in the middle of the living room with a Telecaster plugged into a small Fender amplifier, staring at a big ancient painting of some scene from Greek mythology that belongs to my grandma. I wonder if the artist thought the story was true and why he and countless others like him thought these stories were important enough to tell.

I look down from the painting at the fabric of one of my grandma's rugs under my bare feet. I smile because she's everywhere around me here and as I sink into the moment, I get lost in the same woven patterns I used to stare at when I was a little kid lying on this rug in her living room. Scarlett's pictures start running through the colors and the reminders of love seem reassuring, like a safe place where Scarlett can breathe. Kind of like this rug was to me back then.

I start to play chords that feel like coming home and before long I have the skeleton of a song but no vocal melody. So I turn down the volume knob on the guitar, turn off the amp, and head upstairs to call Jordan.

He's just moved back to San Diego from Nashville with his wife and toddler son. They want to be closer to family and friends now, because her belly is already swollen with another one on the way. When they come over the next day to say hello I play Jordan my idea on the guitar and he sits with his eyes closed and sings and re-sings a melody until he finds what he's looking for. After they leave I sing his melody with the words I've written about the photos in Scarlett's letter and they fit together perfectly, like we'd come up with everything at the same time, and almost a year to the day after the shooting I'll find myself playing "So You Would Know" for Scarlett in a SoHo apartment in New York City, my hands shaking as they hold the guitar, the moment captured by a small recorder left on the table.

But there's something left undone, a song of celebration I'd wanted to write before I got sidetracked by "So You Would Know," so the next morning I go through the pages of letters to find the first one to me from Scarlett, where she says she thought of Jesse as a song for which God gave her the melody and she helped with the words. I take those words, like determination and grace and courage, and wrap my own words around them and show the lyrics to Molly. I ask her to come up with a melody, a waltz that Jesse and Scarlett could dance to, and within a couple of days we have "Celebration (Scarlett's Song)" done.

We record it live downstairs and as Molly sings I realize I've framed the song around God without any of my usual resistance to that kind of thing. I stand with my guitar around my neck, waiting for my part to come toward the end of the song and as the song builds I can hear a darkness that feels like it is there to honor this different kind of celebration. I close my eyes and start to play chords and I see Scarlett in a field of wildflowers. To her that field is God and turning to God seems to be better for the world than turning to hate, and by the time we're all in at the end I know it doesn't matter what I think about God anyway, it matters what Scarlett thinks about God.

Because this song is for Jesse, this is Scarlett's song.

*   *   *

celebration (scarlett's song)

i would write these words
and put them in a frame
to hang in God's kitchen
when he calls your name

grace beauty light love

strength courage determination

i would write these words
and put them in a song
a soundtrack to your life
for the world to sing along

celebration
celebration
celebration

and now that your time has come
now that your time has come
now that your time has come
i can see clearly

i already wrote the words
against His melody
grateful for the music
God has given me
with my pen and His guitar
your life became a song
i will always love you Jesse
i will always sing along

celebration
celebration
celebration

*   *   *

After everyone leaves I listen back to "Celebration" and then "Bullet," and there's something different about the singing and playing in the songs. I can almost hear that twenty-something grams they say disappears when a body dies, the difference in weight between blood and bone and life and only blood and bone, what Scarlett and I talk about on the phone that day I get her letter. I think it's here in these songs somewhere, a spark of what makes us human, and by the time I hear Molly's voice again at the end of "Bullet," I know it.

Maybe this tragedy will spark a flame that somehow shines a light on the world's deficit just like Scarlett writes in her letter, a light like Dante's fire of voices rising up to the heavens in *Paradiso*, the last third of his epic work of deliverance: *From a little spark may burst a flame.*

And I hope with these three songs that a picture has been painted of Jesse and Scarlett, one of many pictures hanging in a beautiful gallery, full of soft light streaming through the windows, where we as a nation spent time grieving and celebrating all that was and is Sandy Hook Elementary School.

And where Scarlett still sits, alone on a museum bench, staring at her canvas with a quiet smile.

I let go of the reins and drape them across the horse's back and her body softens. I stare at the fence rail, still thinking about the cowboy saying, and then glance back at her. She's staring right at me and although the small flicker of something asking to come out in her eyes has already been extinguished by the diesel engine backfire, there's a new softness there.

Her ears are set forward and all four hooves are evenly spaced, still anchoring legs that are ready to move quickly if she feels the need to run. I walk past the horse to get the lead rope hanging on the fence rail and her head turns, and then her chest turns, and as I pass by she takes a couple of steps toward me. A tinge of uneasiness shoots through me because I don't know what she's doing and I stop walking so I can jump to the side if she's planning to run me over.

But when I stop, she stops. I take another few steps away from her and she again takes a few steps with me. I wonder if there's something wrong with her because this horse who won't let me on her back can't be willing to walk with me on her own. But she does, she walks slowly, her neck at my hip, step-by-step with her head relaxed, out the arena gate and down the gravel road as we make our way back to her stall.

I'm not sure what it means and can't quite believe it's happening. I slow my walk in response to a wave from a man watching his daughter ride in the arena and the horse glides to a stop just behind me. He asks why the horse is staying with me even though I'm not holding the reins and before I can answer *I don't know* he says he can't remember ever seeing that sort of thing outside an arena.

Just then she extends her neck and gently places her muzzle in the crease under my arm where my shoulder meets my back and she doesn't nudge me, she only rests her nose there gently. The man says *Ain't that a special thing* and *How did you train her to do that?* and keeps talking but I can't hear him because I'm hearing the horse. I know in my mind that horses can't talk but I also know that something somewhere is saying *I got hurt and I have wounds that need to heal and I know you aren't trying to hurt me and I will get better.* I stand there thinking I may be making more of this than I should be but I don't believe I am.

Sometimes the smallest moments are the biggest and if this man wasn't still talking and asking questions and answering them himself I would probably be crying quietly into my coat right here next to this horse, a horse that I now see has some sort of beautiful fire inside of her but needs help bringing it out, like we all sometimes do when faced with change we know to be true and necessary but still find so hard to bear.

THE STEP

A journey of a thousand miles begins with a single step.

— LAO TZU

Me and my dad

U

This one small step is as difficult for the horse to make as a giant leap over a canyon. It's a step backward into what she fears the most, which is anything in the space above and behind her head. And I'm here, sitting high on the fence rail behind her. She's not willing to trust that I won't hurt her from up here, because someone probably did, so she's not moving even an inch backward to me. Her right hind hoof is firmly planted so she can push off from it and escape past the tall woman in the wide-brimmed hat and chaps holding the lead rope right in front of her.

The tall woman isn't really a horse trainer. She doesn't teach them to jump over crossbars or run courses or race quarter miles, although she has almost done it all, which is why she now will do none of it. But she does teach horses and humans how to help each other and reminds me of a long-dead Irish man I read about whose gift was a nontraditional rehabilitation of horses, especially for his time. He was secretive about his actual methods but to the people who saw him work it looked as if he stood so close to the horse that he was whispering to it.

So if there's such a thing as a horse whisperer, that's her.

I find her through a friend who invites me to watch her work with a troubled horse out at the barn and as she calms a huge rearing Warmblood down into a puddle in a matter of minutes I wonder if maybe she could help my horse and me. So I get the horse from her stall and bring her to the woman and she looks at the horse and I can tell she sees and understands something that I can see but can't understand. After spending a few minutes walking around with the horse she says *Yes, we can do something here.*

She tells me that there's something very special about the horse, something that got pushed down by a human in a way we'll probably never know but something we can maybe bring back out. So we begin with what we do know, which is that the horse has been ridden with a severe shank bit in her mouth. The woman says shank bits force a lot of leverage on a horse's mouth and can cause a lot of pain in sensitive horses if they aren't used right.

And this horse is very sensitive the woman says. *They aren't all very sensitive, but this horse is as sensitive as it gets.* So she'll try a gentler snaffle bit, which will feel so much lighter to the horse that she may think that there's hardly anything there at the other end of the reins to hold her back.

A small crowd gathers at the barn to watch the woman climb on the horse for the first time after she slips the gentler bit into the horse's mouth. The woman eases into the saddle and she's barely seated when the horse takes off at a full gallop toward the far fence line like she did the first time I got on her. She looks like a runaway horse and those watching from the fence hold their breath and a few gasp as the horse and rider approach the first turn way too fast for something bad not to happen.

But the horse stays upright as she rounds the corner and unlike me the woman stays on in the middle of this hurricane, lightly pulling on one of the reins every few strides and asking the horse *Could you let that thought go? Could you?* After what seems like one long tangled blur of speed the horse comes to a stop and breathes in and out heavily and lifts her tail high and snorts and somehow this woman is still on her, this woman who understands her and reaches down across the horse's sweaty shoulder and caresses her neck and leans into her ear and whispers *Well, that was interesting.*

Not long after the January performance at the theater a local TV news anchor tells me he wants to do a documentary about *For the Sender.* We go back and forth on e-mail and he asks me to check out his son Graham's music and I do and tell him that Graham just needs to keep playing and writing and getting whatever's inside of him out because he's good and you never know what can happen. Maybe he will be luckier than me, luckier than most of us walking this line between what we love to do and what it costs.

In one of the e-mails he calls me Eric and over the next few days he continues a conversation with me thinking I'm someone else. When he realizes the mistake he says he's losing his mind and I say *You're right, you're losing your mind* but I don't know at the time that he really is. Maybe he doesn't know yet either, maybe he doesn't know that he will go from wanting to do a story about *For the Sender* to actually being a story in it. But he sends me an e-mail of explanation, his words typed by his daughter because it's hard for him to write now that brain cancer has taken hold and left him with precious little time and hands that don't always work.

The letter is about leaving nothing out on the field when he has to go, not leaving any songs unsung, paraphrased in a great quote from Hunter S. Thompson. And as I read I think maybe the cancer has taken hold of his hands but it will be long after the end before it could ever take his spirit. Which it never will.

*   *   *

Dear Alex,

For the Sender had me from the opening pages. The idea of heartfelt prose inspiring music touched my spirit. As a journalist, I hoped to follow and to share that magic. And without knowing it, there was a deeper and more personal purpose in the project. On January 29, 2013, terminal cancer made a participant of an observer.

It's peculiar how brain cancer has altered my perception of time. Suddenly, time takes on new meaning —and it's not a bad thing. No moment is wasted and there's no room to dwell on the negative. A meaningful life awaits and it will be devoted to opening my eyes in those ways I have been unable—until now. I don't want to miss another sunset, another milestone in my kids' lives. Along the way I want to laugh, listen to music, and explore every facet of this life.

"Life should not be a journey to the grave with the intention of arriving safely in a pretty and well-preserved body, but rather to skid in broadside in a cloud of smoke, thoroughly used up, totally worn out, and loudly proclaiming 'Wow! What a ride!'" — Hunter S. Thompson

Loren

*   *   *

The quote at the end of Loren's letter reminds me of the words *don't die with your music still in you*, words I remember from a public-television special I saw years ago, words for deeper living that I wrote down on the back of a yellow flyer I used to promote a show no one came to. It's been over a decade since then so I doubt I still have the flyer but I look for it anyway and within a few minutes I find it tucked in the pocket of a notebook full of lyrics and memories, buried in the bottom drawer of my desk.

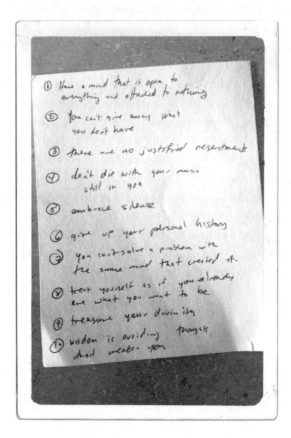

I read the ten suggestions again and these are good ideas, reminders I could tape to a mirror and look at every day and maybe live better by. And as I read, I can hear the voice from the public-television special delivering these words. A deep, knowing voice. A voice I recognize from sometime in the last few weeks, a voice I've just heard in New York.

∪

I'm playing a show down in San Diego a couple of weeks later and in a scrape of serendipity Loren's son, Graham, happens to be the opener on the bill. I watch him and his band roll through a solid country set as I stand next to Loren, his right hand occasionally bracing his body against the bar table. But he's here, he's standing, stepping side to side, clapping and yelling at the end of every song as his kid takes a cue from his dad by not leaving his own songs unsung.

I look to my left and see Dan and his family sitting in one of the booths off to the side of the stage. I walk over to say hello and thanks for coming and I tell him we've just finished the songs about his letters and he says he can't wait to hear them. It's time for me to play so I head back toward the stage thinking that maybe Dan being here in the same room as Loren is another compass arrow so before I go on I ask Loren if he has anything he'd like me to write a song about.

A couple of weeks later he sends me a note he's written to Graham, an emailed response to a gig invitation. What do you say to your son when you know your days are short? If you're Loren you say *Hell, yes, let's live for the day and get as far down this road as we can.* Even if Graham has to drive all day and through the night, that's okay. Loren and Hunter S. Thompson will be in the backseat, breathing the night air deep and looking at the stars.

*   *   *

G,

The text from you was unexpected: Bonsai Show May 11 at the Flower Fields. Wanna hang?

Wow—and hell, yes!

You have always been our wild child—an artist whose roots dig deep and whose branches stretch bravely toward the sun. And you've allowed me to bask in the most awe-inspiring elements of your creativity. Being among the crowd at your shows just feels natural—but your enthusiasm to explore my world as you build your own is incredible.

Where our spirits converge, at nature and art, yields a magnetic energy that we have time to explore. And we'll navigate it together—but you'll have to drive.

Your energy and presence are those of an oak tree. I envision you among the hardwood of a great California forest. The extraordinarily deep roots. The impressive strength to grow big and tall. The ability to sustain those around you. And the offering of protection from the sometimes harsh environment. You are the oak. The proud. The sturdy. The true.

Each song you write. Each story you tell. I learn more about you on a deeper level. And there hasn't been a layer yet that has failed to impress me more than the layer before.

I love you, kid.

Dad

*　　*　　*

I read the words *I love you* and think about how my parents hardly ever tell me they love me with the words *I love you* but I've never doubted for a moment that they do. The sacrifices they've made for me and the planning and all the small but important things they've done for me all my life tell me louder than words. When Loren talks about coming to hear Graham's band I see a flash of an image from my past in aged 8-millimeter-film memory. Then another flash, and another. There isn't a continuous scene of movement, only moments from the same scene like weathered photographs strung together on a clothes-line between buildings.

In one picture moment my dad is picking me up from school at lunchtime when all the other kids are eating, and in the next moment we are in the Jack in the Box drive-through ordering a plain cheeseburger because that's how I like it and in the next moment we're taking slow, careful steps on the jetty of rocks jutting out from the harbor in my hometown. My dad is carrying fishing poles and holding my hand and I'm carrying the lunches and we sit on the rocks and eat and stick the poles in the water and the string of photograph moments ends and I say a silent thank you to my own dad as I sit on my couch with Loren's letter in my hands.

I've just put the horse back in her stall and I'm walking to my truck when I hear a thud somewhere behind me. I turn to see a big brown quarterhorse, far heavier than my horse, piled on top of a young girl in the riding arena. This horse isn't moving at all and there's no noise, only the strange quiet calm that occurs when time slows down on the back end of tragedy. I walk softly toward the horse to see the girl pinned under the half-ton animal and I know some part of the girl must be broken. She's only now starting to realize the situation and begins crying quietly, slowly escalating her soft cries louder and louder.

But the big brown horse is perfectly still, almost like a huge carcass that still has blood rushing through its veins and breath in its lungs and somehow understands that if it moves it will hurt the girl. I wrap my arms around the horse's neck and shoulder and with the two other people in the arena I start to roll the animal away from and off the girl, expecting a panic of movement from the horse and a flailing kick into the girl's flesh or my own.

But there is none. Not a muscle on the horse twitches. After what seems to be an eternity we have the horse lifted enough to pull the girl out and somehow in the miraculous cluster of moments the girl gets up on her own and walks around and has no broken bones, not even a sprain that we can see. We stand looking at the big brown horse, still motionless on the ground but blinking and breathing, and we wonder silently, each of us knowing what the other is thinking, if the horse has broken its leg or its back and will have to be put down.

And then like a foal struggling to its feet for the first time, the horse pushes up onto its front legs, and with shaking, quivering muscles he stands. He stands in front of us in all of his power and grace and understanding and we're humbled to tears because before us is presence as a gift, this presence that knows it can hurt us and chooses not to.

I approach him gently and take one of his reins and we walk a few steps and he doesn't seem to be lame. The girl limps over to me and asks if she can take him back to his stall and I give her the reins and watch as she gingerly walks with the horse out of the arena. I wonder if that's what I looked like that first day after I fell off my own horse, not fifteen feet from where we're standing now.

Later that afternoon I talk to the man who owns the big brown horse and I tell him how I was looking in the horse's eye while he was laying on the girl and I saw something deep and ancient and knowing there. The man says it's like looking into the eye of a whale, where we can see beauty and grace and restrained calm behind this incredible power. It's a vastness of spirit greater than we understand, a presence we have to slow down to experience. And a gift, in her unbroken bones and breath of life, that the young girl will likely remember forever.

I invite Graham over to the house to see how we get along and if we can write a song together. He's a big, likable kid and we start playing guitars and talking about his dad and the diagnosis and I tell him that lately I've been thinking about my own mortality and how I know that I'm going to go someday, how we're all going to go, it's just that his dad kind of knows when he's going to go. And the irony is I could get hit by a car tonight walking my dog and go before his dad does, nobody ever knows when it's coming. We talk about how maybe it's a gift to have the awareness that this kind of death sentence brings because it encourages broad, deep, loving steps down the still-sunlit path with a new understanding of how precious the moment is.

But really we should all be taking those kinds of steps, because all of our days are short and we never know when the road may end.

Graham goes to Yosemite with his dad in a van they've retrofitted to camp in and comes back with the song we've started almost done. We sit down in my living room with our guitars and keep trading words and melodies until "We Ain't Got The Time" shows itself. The vulnerability in the word *daddy* coming from a big kid with a tough exterior makes the song special to me.

The next week he comes over to sing a temporary vocal track as a guide for us to record the instruments because I'm planning on having Jordan sing the song. Loren walks in the house just behind him, even though he's just had a seizure that morning and is finding the smallest of moments much more difficult now. At first he stays in the hall because he hasn't heard the whole song and doesn't know how he'll react, but between tears and a small smile he makes his way between the drums and guitar amps over to the couch where the tears get smaller and the smile gets bigger as he watches his son. Five feet away Graham is singing a song to him and for him as we all play and it's then that I decide I will keep Graham's voice on the song as a record of all this moment is between a father and his son, this precious and sacred and slowly closing window of time.

recording with Graham while Loren and his daughters watch

*   *   *

we ain't got the time

hey dad i got your letter
and i ain't much of a writer
so i'll sing you a song
i've seen big ships pull out of nasty weather
rock back and forth and sail on

The Step

and now there's a storm moving through
tell me dad what's a boy to do

not gonna lie this don't sit well
and it hurts my heart to see you go through hell
i say my prayers every night in my bed
when the heaps of thoughts run through my head
don't cry
we got a life to live

thank you for bringing me up right
you always seem to know just what i need
i owe you one for bailing me out of trouble that night
yeah I'm a wild one but you planted the seed

there ain't nothing i could do
to show appreciation for a friend like you

not gonna lie this don't sit well
and it hurts my heart to see you go through hell
i say my prayers every night in my bed
when the heaps of thoughts run through my head
don't cry
we got a life to live
we got a life to live

daddy please don't cry
we ain't got the time

not gonna lie this don't sit well
and it hurts my heart to see you go through hell
i say my prayers every night in my bed
when the heaps of thoughts run through my head
don't cry
we got a life to live

*   *   *

A friend sends me a controversial documentary that at first seems to be about God and religion. As I watch the first few minutes of the movie my mind wanders off into a field, similar to the field I imagined with Scarlett while playing her song, but on one side of this field is God and on the other side is religion. The God side is wind rustling through the wildflowers and tall mountain grasses and the religion side is a huge church built of steel and concrete that's cut into earth now devoid of green. They're in the same field but they're not the same thing, and maybe whatever resistance I have left to using the word *God* in these songs isn't really about the wild side of the field, maybe it's more about the side severed with this man-made construct of walls over which wars are waged and behind which all that is inescapably human will always dwell.

I come back to the movie in time to hear the narrator suggest that many of history's central religious figures share similar stories because they were fabricated based on the same entity: the sun. Ancient cultures wanted to honor the sun because they depended on it for everything good, like warmth and planting season and the grace of light after the dark, dangerous night. So they attributed the sun's characteristics and movements to a god, a solar messiah they could worship. And now I understand why this movie is controversial, it's because it claims that Jesus is also a solar messiah, a religious figurehead whose story is based on the sun.

About a third of the way through I turn off the TV and get up from the couch, not convinced but kind of intrigued. Maybe Jesus did exist as a man, a spiritual teacher, and then after his death the stories about him took on those of mythic solar messiahs. I don't know, and none of us were there, so none of us really know. It does get me thinking though.

I remember a pastor coming on television a few Sundays before and I don't want to watch a well-manicured white man ask for money so I begin looking for the remote to change the channel. I stop looking for the remote when I hear him say *True love is seen in what you do*. The pastor reads a few Bible verses and says that before Jesus did any healing or ministering or anything like that, he went around doing good to people. The rest of the sermon is spent telling these stories of Jesus doing good to people and of ordinary people giving to each other and the pastor says again that this is what true love is. What we do for others.

I turn off the TV thinking that I don't have a church with a steeple or a cross or a pulpit or a pew but that doesn't mean I can't believe in what Jesus did and had to say. I could care less if he came out of a virgin or a cow or a hooker or if somebody just made him up. If he talked about doing good to each other and looking out for your brother, he talked about love as something you do. I can believe in that.

And now the more I start to see Jesus as a mythical figure, not as a real person, the more I actually start to believe in him. Because if I can believe in the mythical Jesus and his stories and teachings, I don't have to believe in the existence of an actual person who really was born from a virgin and who really walked on water and who really turned water into wine. I only have to believe in his message and the power of his stories.

I can hear my friend Jon laughing outside on the street and I look out the front window to see him and his dad pulling on their wetsuits and getting ready to surf. His dad is also a pastor and I've never been to his church but I like him a lot and want to hear him speak there someday. Maybe he stands more on the side of the field where the wind blows through the pines than on the side with the towering walls of concrete.

And when he talks about Jesus and the Bible, I wonder if he talks about the blood and bone of the man and the typeface used in the book or if he talks more about the lessons and truths found in the stories of Jesus and those who came before him, stories by which generations have communicated with each other long before Christianity was a spark in anyone's heart.

One of my favorite books is the Tao Te Ching by Lao Tzu, which came along more than five centuries before Jesus was born. I remember reading the thirteenth verse of the Tao where Lao Tzu says *Love the world as yourself* and then scrambling to find a Bible because it sounded like something Jesus would say. Which he did, over five hundred years later somewhere in the book of Matthew. *Thou shalt love thy neighbor as thyself.*

These kinds of lessons are woven into stories that resonate regardless of religion or race or creed, stories of Jesus and Lao Tzu and other teachers, stories forged through the ages in the crucible of human experience and handed down from ancient fathers to today's sons. And maybe this is the real power of these stories, regardless of whether their characters actually existed or not. We've carried them through the centuries because they point to something true.

And I run downstairs, grab my board, and catch up to Jon and his dad before they reach the water.

I recognize him. He cuts a tall figure with a clean-shaven head and speaks with a deep, knowing voice that I remember, a voice that somehow calms and inspires at the same time and this is the voice telling me not to die with my music still in me from the public-television special I saw in my twenties. I remember wondering how he could know that music really is what I have inside me and thinking *No, I don't want to die with it still in there.*

The same voice now tells me backstage at an event where our paths have crossed that he's read my book and listened to my songs and thinks what I'm doing is wonderful. And when I say *We'll see where it goes* he looks at me, not really me, but more my blood and heart and says *It will go where you want it to go.* He's one of the world's most respected teachers of life's biggest lessons so I don't argue even though I'm not sure that what I want for me is always what's best.

A mutual friend pulls me aside and tells me that reading my words has inspired this teacher's next book about looking back on his life. My breath catches because I don't expect to hear this at all. And I want to honor it somehow so, through the friend, I ask the teacher if I can write a song for him, maybe about one of the reflections in his new book.

He doesn't answer with reflections but instead sends me a letter written to him by one of his daughters, Serena. Serena's words to her father weave their own kind of religion into a narrative more about God and what God means and dharma, and I don't even know what that means but I think it must have to do with doing what you are supposed to be doing, and I hope I'm fulfilling my dharma, too.

*   *   *

Dad,

Today I sat behind you in Ephesus, Turkey, while you gave a lecture to a few hundred people who had traveled from all over the world to hear you speak. I was overcome with emotion as I saw you standing there, ful-filling your dharma while touching the lives of so many. I know you as my father, but you have always been a teacher to me as well. You have taught me that the solu-tions to all of life's problems are inside of me, and that I only had to go within, be silent and present, and know that all is well.

You never told me how to live or what to think or what to believe in. Instead, you showed me how to make each step a prayer and each word a word of love. You taught me to believe in magic and miracles, and you showed me how to be in awe of the awesome world we live in.

Since the time I was brought into this world, I knew that I was safe to be exactly as I was, and that whoever I was, I was a perfect creation of God. You told me that I was God, and that it was God that looks out from behind my eyes. I learned from you that I was master of my own fate, the creator of my destiny.

Of all the lessons I have learned, the thing that hit me hardest was when you said that I am God. Could I really be a spark of God, a perfect creation put here on Earth with a purpose? You say this all the time, but I have always struggled with it, especially since school and society were telling me otherwise. I doubted myself, felt inferior, and worried that I needed to apologize to someone for even contemplating this idea. I have felt unworthy, undeserved, and unsure. Although you gave me great tools, I still had to figure out how to use them on my own. Now I understand that God is love, God is beauty, and God is truth. You told me I came from an infinite space of perfection and that I will return to it one day, too. Slowly I am beginning to understand.

People love you so much and yet to me you have always been Dad. You drove me to school each morning, you taught me how to swim and ride a bike, you read me stories, and you came to all my plays. As I have grown, you have encouraged me to follow my dharma and go after whatever it is that excites me. You believe in me, Dad, and I love you so much for that.

What do you say to someone who gave you life and then showed you how to live it? You say thank you, thank you, thank you.

I Love You,
Serena

*   *   *

I notice the sentence about Serena receiving not only the gift of life from her dad but also the gift of learning how to live it, and I'm reminded of Dan's letter to Frank where Dan says that Frank gave him the gift of showing him how to die. Both are beautiful gifts, the learning how to live and the learning how to die. So I write a song called "This Gift" about the ultimate gratitude in Serena's letter and ask one of her sisters, Skye, if she would like to sing it to their dad onstage sometime at an event we may be at together.

She says yes and before the season turns we are onstage when midway through the song her dad reaches his hand out to her as she sings and I watch her take one step after another in slow motion and take his hand and his eyes well with tears and I can't keep watching and play guitar at the same time. I look down at my hands until I play the last chord and he wraps his arms around me and says *Thank you*, and these two small words have more weight than all the volumes in all the world's libraries.

*   *   *

this gift

first words talking
first steps walking

FOR THE SENDER: LOVE IS (NOT A FEELING)

those times i don't recall

every stage at
every play i know
you were there for them all

and i know sometimes
people thank you
for God's gift you showed they had
but this time
i want to thank you
for this gift of being my dad

as i got older
if dreams would smolder
you helped bring back the fire

to warm my cold night
through the firelight
my spark of God flew higher
i know sometimes
people thank you
for God's gift you showed they had
but this time
i want to thank you
for this gift of being my dad

i know as time goes by

you will be watching
from my first steps
to my last

but they won't be our last

because we together
walk forever
now from future into past

so i love that
people thank you
for God's gift you showed they had
but this time
i want to thank you
i want to thank you
i love you dad

*   *   *

The horse is focused intently on a blue tarp flapping in the wind to her right, her neck stiff and tense and her mind ready to tell her body to flee. I gently pull on the left rein and say *Could you let that thought go?* and the pressure on the rein turns her attention to the left, away from the perceived danger of the tarp, and toward me. Within a couple of seconds her head drops and she lets out a deep, relaxed sigh and I can feel the tension drain through her feet and out of her body.

This is the question the woman was asking the horse on their first whirlwind ride together and it's the better question I'd been looking for a few months ago, when I was asking my *whys* in frustration as the horse answered by spinning circles around me.

The woman has shown me that whenever the horse becomes worried about something I can help her let go of the anxiety by asking her to turn her attention away from whatever's worrying her, with a rein or the lead rope or my body language. So both my questions and her answers are about letting go, they are mirrors to each other, kind of like the cowboy saying.

Every chance I get I bring the horse to the woman and we slowly begin to deconstruct the horse's past without knowing the shape or color of it, only what we discover and share from our experiences with her. In the process of registering the horse as her new owner, the voice on the other end of the phone tells me that her sire was one of the most famous horses in her breed, a two-time world champion and sire to many other world champions.

I don't know what this means or if it matters but the woman believes that because the horse's dad was famous she was likely used more for breeding and less for riding. When she had delivered enough foals to make some money she was trained up quickly, and probably with force given the way she's fallen apart, in order to sell her fast. The woman says some horses can almost handle that kind of aggressive training, although she doesn't agree with it and stresses the "almost" and tells me that the wrong kind of training turns a horse this sensitive into a ticking time bomb, with fear and anxiety and worry held in under pressure to avoid pain.

One afternoon when we're done working I tell the woman about the time the horse drags me a good twenty feet on the ground, twenty feet I'm grateful for because that's when in the blood and dirt I finally find what's missing.

It's a few months earlier and I'm leading the horse around an obstacle course with old rubber tires meant to maneuver her through and big wooden pallets meant for her to stand on and other man-made artificial challenges meant to simulate the real world. Side by side, we approach a suspended metal rod with pieces of flexible plastic hanging down, like the giant washrags in an automated car wash. I don't know when we'll be going through a car wash in the real world but we walk under it anyway.

The horse's head is low, which means she's relaxed, something that's become a little more common now when I'm on the ground with her. She doesn't mind the plastic brushing against her muzzle and ears as we pass under the rod, even as her whole head is engulfed by the pieces of plastic, so I let out the breath I've been holding and walk forward with her.

Her head clears the rod and I hear the hanging pieces of plastic rustle and shift as they fall back into place above and behind her and in that instant her neck stiffens and arches and she takes off running as fast as her legs can carry her. The rope immediately tightens in my hand and my first instinct is to hang on and before I can think or do anything else I'm being dragged like a buoy behind a boat. A really fast boat.

It takes me a second to figure out that I have to let go. As soon as I do the horse stops and I lay there on the ground looking at my forearm, raw almost to the bone from the friction between earth and skin. I turn my head up to her and she's looking at me like she looked at me that day I fell, like she doesn't know what just happened. And at first I don't either, but as I start to push myself up it hits me.

She doesn't run when the plastic pieces are coming at her muzzle, or falling all around her head, or even passing over her ears. But the moment the plastic pieces are making noise above and behind her head, some kind of fear takes over and she throws her head in the air and runs.

So at some point something bad must have happened to her, something that came from above and behind her head, and laying there on the ground I realize that this is where a rider would sit. Someone must have done something that hurt her or scared her while they were riding her. As I get to my knees I close my eyes and see her taking off with me that first day I got her, I see the wounds on her belly from the over-tightened cinch, I see her now spinning around and trying as hard as she can not to allow me to get on her. I see all of that set against her calmer and gentler way of being when I'm on the ground, and it all makes perfect sense.

She doesn't want me up there because she doesn't trust anything up there.

And that's how I find what's missing there in the dirt. Trust.

My belief moves to knowing later in the fall. With the help of the woman, the horse has started allowing me on her back and I'm riding her down a dirt road, talking to her quietly and noticing how she's more relaxed than usual, when a bee flies under the brim of my hat. I don't want to get stung so I quickly reach for the brim and pull the hat off my head and the horse bolts down the road. I stay on her until she calms down to a walk and I put my hat back on and wave my hand in the same motion over her ears and she doesn't bolt. I do this over and over, switching between waving my hand holding the hat and waving an empty hand, and her reaction alternates between calm and fear accordingly and this is our breakthrough, this is how my belief moves to knowing that someone beat her with something in their hand.

So the woman and I work on getting the horse comfortable with movement and noises above and behind her head and we spend days helping the horse understand that she has little to fear when she's with me and that she can actually find support here. These days of two steps up and one step back lead to beautiful moments that carry me long after I leave the barn and I drive home one early evening thinking that I could fill a book with what I learn about myself and the horse.

But the harder questions about really deep trust, like this one the woman is asking the horse right now as I sit high on the fence rail behind her, still go unanswered.

The woman eases her hold on the lead rope after she asks the horse one more time *Could you trust him and take a step backward?*

I smile at the *could you* because when I'm carrying the weight of heavier thoughts from a future I can't predict or a past I can't change, it's not the horse I hear the woman talking to, it's me. I can hear her even now, as I'm caught in an unexpected tangle of worry, asking me *Could you let that thought go?*

Well, could you?

One thought I can't let go is the image of my dad and me taking those steps over the rocks the day he picked me up from elementary school and took me to get a plain cheeseburger and then fishing. I've written a song with Graham about his dad and seen for myself their closing window and written a song of thanks to the teacher from his daughter, but there's another song I need to write. And sing.

Which I do, alone except for a big brown dog who gets up from wherever she is at the end of the song and reaches her neck up over the piano bench to lick my tears when they come. Which they do.

*   *   *

who i come from

so you want to know something about me
what kind of man you can expect me to be
will i stand right here beside you faithfully

some pictures are worth more than words

there's a photo over there where the light's shining down
on a rental tuxedo and worn wedding gown
his promise was forever when this city was a town

that photo on the wall
of who I come from
can answer any question at all

so what if i got a decision
between drinking and fishing with him
will i hold his hand by the ocean if he don't swim

some pictures are worth more than words
there's another one there before you hit the door
he's holding my hand as I stumble down the shore
i think we're going fishing he knows it's something more

those photos on the wall
of who I come from
can answer any question at all

now if that don't tell you something
about the song I'm gonna sing
take another look over there darling

there's a photo over there where the light's shining down
on my daddy's tuxedo and mama's wedding gown
his promise was forever he never backed down

and there's another one there before you hit the door
he's holding my hand as I stumble down the shore
i think we're going fishing he knows it's something more

those photos on the wall
of who I come from
can answer any question at all

if you want to know something about me
what kind of man you can expect me to be

*   *   *

A few weeks later I play the song for him as he and my mom sit on the couch, finally able to breathe deep quiet breaths after the last of their guests have left. It's the tail end of their fiftieth wedding-anniversary celebration and until now the house has been full of comings and goings and the gentle chaos of family and friends and my mom says many of them never thought my parents would make it this far. But of course what other people think about what may or may not happen means nothing. They made it.

And now it's only my mom and dad and the woman I wrap my arms around and they listen as I stumble through the song, the woman disappearing a couple of times around the corner to the kitchen so no one sees her cry. I wonder if my dad is understanding what the song is about, if he gets it, and by the time I play the last chord my mom has wet eyes and my dad stares straight ahead and wonders out loud if we went fishing that day or if we just walked along the rocks.

He gets it.

The horse is still an arm's length away from my knees as I sit above and behind her on the fence. Just before the woman asks the horse for the last time to take a step back she says again that even the tiniest movement of the horse's right hind hoof backward toward me would be a significant sign of trust, because she'd be deciding on her own to take a small step back toward something she fears. And a very real step toward believing she has nothing to fear at all.

This is almost too much to handle for a horse whose mistrust runs as deep as hers does, so we have to honor even the slightest effort that she might make. The woman says that asking the horse to jump over a canyon or lie down in front of us in full submission would be just as difficult for her as this small step backward.

But the hoof is still anchored in the dirt and no number of eyes watching the hoof will ever make it move, no amount of human hope or belief will ever make it move, no gentle pressure on her halter will make it move, nothing but this massive animal who is refusing to let go and believe and trust will ever make it move.

And then the horse gently tentatively slowly releases her anchor and picks up her right hind hoof and we watch to see if it will move forward away from me in distrust or if it will move backward toward me in trust. The hoof hangs in the air, suspended between the two as we all are sometimes, caught between momentous shifts in the smallest of moments.

And gently tentatively slowly, a few inches from where she picks it up, Annie places her hoof back down in the dirt. Backward, to me.

THE FIELD

Out beyond ideas of wrongdoing and rightdoing
there is a field. I'll meet you there.

— RUMI

Christian and Sidney

U

The late-season San Diego rain is dripping down the back of my shirt as I take Annie from her stall just before daybreak and load her into the horse trailer. Stella is already in the backseat of the truck and by 5:30 on this wet June morning I'm pulling all of us away to the mountains of southern Idaho, far from the ocean of humans and buildings and cars spilling over the edges of Southern California. The draw toward space and wild has become stronger as my circle of friends in San Diego continues to scatter farther so I've found a place to live for the summer at the foot of a towering butte with acres of fenced pasture for Annie surrounded by lodgepole pines and gently sloping hills crawling up into the rugged Smoky Mountains.

We pull into the field close to midnight and I fumble by starlight with the trailer latch to open the rear door. I step up into the trailer saying *It's okay, it's okay* as I run my hand from Annie's tail up her spine to her head, where I take the halter hanging on my arm and wrap it gently around her neck and muzzle and slowly turn her to the back of the trailer, which is now open to the wild. She steps hesitantly out of the trailer and into the field, where I shut the gate in the fence behind us and take her halter off and wait to see what she does. She stands next to me for a moment and then in a silent explosion bursts into the night, away across the field until the blur of her legs is lost in the black.

I wake the next morning to see her standing at the fence outside my bedroom window, looking up at the house for some sign of life. I stumble down to the barn in my pajamas and she nickers low and deep as I pull some hay from the three-ton stock stacked behind her shed and throw it over the fence. She lowers her head and pushes around the alfalfa and orchard grass until she finds a place to start eating and that simple ritual of feeding is the beginning of a deeper kind of connection to land and animal, one forged by dirt under fingernails and clothing full of dust, impossible to wash away because it's the stuff of life.

A few days later I walk out to the field where Annie has stopped anxiously pacing the fenceline in her search for some sense of familiarity. There's nothing familiar to her here but me and I wish I could tell her that all that's new must and will become familiar: the screech of the magpie call, the pungent smell of sheep herded up the canyon, the dry breath of mountain wind tumbling down the pass, all this and more will become familiar to her, and this can only be with time.

But now that she's stopped walking the fence I think maybe it's time to put a saddle on her, so I throw the twenty-five pounds of leather onto her back and gently slide the metal bit into her mouth and she offers little resistance. I remember what happened the last time I climbed on her in a new environment so I call over the fence to my neighbor and ask her to help just in case. I ask her to hold the reins and she does with legs spread wide and feet firmly planted in front of Annie as if she's holding back a rocket ship from liftoff. I step into the stirrup and swing my leg over the cantle and sit down gently and my neighbor asks *What do I do?* and I say *Let go I guess.*

She lets go and Annie stands there. She doesn't take off running or trotting or even walking. She just stands there and I close my eyes and say a silent please and give her a small nudge with my legs, but she still stands there. I give her a firmer nudge, then a firmer one, until she finally takes one plodding step after another and we circle the three acre field at a slow walk.

My neighbor says *She looks fine to me* and she feels different under me than in the days before we left California, calmer with less worry. As I climb off her I think maybe it's the trust born in our small moments together or maybe it's because she can move at her own pace now through the worry and the sage and lupine and aspen trees scattered across her field, as she does the afternoon I call to her from a quarter mile away and for the first time she lifts and turns her head toward me, sets her ears forward and walks, then trots, then runs and skids to a stop an arm's length from my unshaven face.

The gravel under my tires settles in front of a big wooden barn held together by a new coat of paint and a sense of quiet calm. There's peace in the wild here, with the Big Wood River framing a couple hundred acres of open Idaho country, dotted with only pastures and barns. A few of some twenty horses raise their heads over the fence at the sound of my truck door closing before returning to more important things, like grass.

I make my way into a converted barn office alive with activity. Little brown and black boots are lined up against one wall, awaiting the feet attached to the bundles of anticipation quietly getting ready in the next room, where conditions and diseases have robbed young voices and silenced young tongues and stiffened young bodies but have not, will not, and will never silence their spirits.

Small helmets are fitted with smaller heads as the barely containable energy in the room struggles to break the confines of these silly protective adults to get out to what matters.

Horses.

What unfolds is beautiful and sad and joyful, as what used to be unmoving now moves and what used to be confused light is now focused energy. Watching one child with a degenerative disease as she is helped onto a horse by two people and some sort of crane and then walked around the arena on the horse with her hands spread wide like she's flying is like watching all of the sun's rays running through a magnifying glass and scorching a pile of paper below, where the paper burning to ash is all this child is unable to do and the sun's rays are her shining life light and the magnifying glass making it all happen is this huge patient understanding animal carrying her from unknowing to knowing to grace.

The place is called Swiftsure Ranch and one of the horses is Sidney and he carries an autistic boy named Christian who is at once inquisitive and violent, sometimes hitting himself with an open hand and trying to destroy whatever's around him before retreating back into a world none of us can truly understand. None of us except maybe for Sidney, a stocky Norwegian Fjord belonging to Brienne, who has built a special bridge of trust between the horse and the people he carries.

Before his time at Swiftsure, Sidney was deeply misunderstood and pushed into a job he wasn't ready for, which caused a bad wreck and in turn made him more anxious. Brienne wanted to save him from this pattern so she took him on as a project and as I touch the animal's muzzle she tells me about a moment between Sidney and

Christian that made her understand more deeply why she's doing this work. It's beautiful and I want to tell whatever world I can reach about this and maybe help Swiftsure somehow so I ask her to write me a letter and she says she will. But she doesn't write me a letter. She doesn't even write a letter to a person. She writes one to her best friend.

*　　*　　*

> *Dear Sidney,*
>
> *Sometimes I'm jealous of you, my friend. Life is so simple for you; the most complication you ever experience is usually brought on by me. You live your life like each day counts and you enjoy the smallest moments, like rolling in the muddiest part of your paddock, yet seem to grasp the profundity of your effect on people. If you didn't somehow understand your students, I couldn't explain how it is that you stand so calmly for one boy who desperately needs your stability, then toss your head and quicken your step for the little girl who needs to laugh. You give yourself so completely to the task at hand, to your special, challenged riders, that I can't believe you don't somehow "get it." You give those students the gifts of your legs, your freedom, and in return you get their hearts. And mine, always and so gratefully, mine.*

Do you remember on Tuesday when we were out on the trail? We were having a great ride; the air felt beautiful and the scenery was fascinating to Christian, the autistic boy you were carrying willingly, even though when he's upset he hits himself hard in the face and can even be violent toward you. You have probably felt me in those moments, placing Christian's palm on your neck and rubbing your mane gently against his hand to soothe him and bring him back to me.

But on Tuesday, out of nowhere, a huge flock of birds flushed right under your face and you (understandably) jumped! It scared all of us, you and Christian included. It was the first time you had ever done anything remotely unsteady while carrying Christian, and I was worried about what would happen. I couldn't believe it when Christian reached down by himself and grabbed a piece of your mane and began rubbing his palm until he was calm and confident again! His first reaction to being upset was to use his friend to soothe himself, not hurt himself! Then you pulled out of your leader's grasp for a moment to turn your big head all the way around and nudge Christian's boot, as if you were apologizing! Since Christian is often apologizing to you, this was a huge moment and he began to laugh when I said, "Lo siento, Christian!" instead of "Lo siento, Sidney," which is what he is used to hearing. I could not have loved you and your boy more if I tried.

I find it so amazing that I'm the "teacher," yet you, who have no voice, often teach more than I ever could. You teach patience and responsibility, kindness and bravery. You teach goodness of heart and strength of character. I might teach people how to ride, but you, dear horse, teach them how to soar.

You've opened my eyes to a new way of learning and understanding relationships and real partnerships. The day I trusted you to carry your first student was the day I realized you were a metaphor for so much in my life. I trust you in your work and you trust me to keep you safe, so you're able to do your work. It's a beautiful circle.

I can't fully express how much I value and appreciate you, how much I love you. You give me words that never have to be spoken to be understood. You give me hope and strength and really only ask for a romp in the field or a carrot or two. Or three. You may never know how many lives you've changed or how much you mean to so many, but that doesn't matter. I know, they know, and it will never be forgotten.

All my love,

B.

*   *   *

That first ride in the field with Annie is followed by cold mountain mornings spent walking down the hill to the small shed that holds her feed and cutting the twine off the fragrant hay bales as she waits at the fence for her breakfast. She wears a deep impression in the dirt outside the shed where she sleeps and lets me scratch her ears as she lies in a mammoth ball like an oversized dog. Every day I feed her and pick up after her and brush her and eat my lunch of apple and peanut-butter sandwiches sitting with my back against her shed's shiplap sides as she grazes a few feet from me. To hear a horse eat, the slow workings of bone against hay, is to hear a lullaby.

We spend our late afternoons riding from the field into some of the most beautiful country on Earth. There's no social media in this country, there's not even media or really anything social either. There are only trees turning green to yellow to orange to red and the echoes of coyote howls, only herds of elk moving across the valley and red-tailed hawks above. There are only calloused fingers fumbling with reins and the smell of ancient earth, only a wild sky under which the rattle and hum of small devices goes unnoticed, unheeded, as it has for ages and will long after we're gone.

As summer begins to weave into fall we head farther into the mountain passes behind her field, where Annie carries me over streams and rocks and gravel and slows her pace to a near crawl on the asphalt road as we come back to the field, showing no sign of concern as the occasional car or bike passes.

I start allowing Stella, my new brown Labrador, to come along for rides with Annie and me. She's not really new, because she's been with me for quite a while, but I didn't like her at first and now that I do she seems new. She's settled down with time and especially since coming to Idaho, but the vestiges of her rambunctious bordering on aggressive tendencies are still there, carried over from the chaos that defined her growing up. I think sometimes we just come out into the world however we come out, and Stella came out on fire.

As a puppy her enthusiastic play devolves into more defensive behavior after she's brutally attacked by a pit bull–ridgeback mix in the parking lot of my apartment complex. She's sitting at my side, barely four months old, when the pit approaches and smells her, moves a few feet away, and then pounces on her. He has her by the neck and before I know what I'm doing I'm punching him as hard as I can anywhere and everywhere. My instinct to protect is so strong that I can't think of anything but to destroy what is destroying something I love and no consequence matters, not my safety or anything else.

After five or six seconds he retreats with his tail between his legs around to the side of the building, but the damage to Stella is done. Like her big sister Annie, Stella will carry the emotional wounds with her long after the stints are removed from her skin and the countless stitches heal. And Stella's instinct to protect will now run as deep as mine.

I call an album I'm working on back then *Up with the Sun* after the early mornings when she whines and scratches and gnaws her way out of the house and into neighbors' plants and yards and lunges after their cats and children. She doesn't back down to bigger dogs, especially after the attack, and has already begun to distribute and collect her own share of scars.

Very little furniture survives that period and a few interior car parts are lost as well and the small apartment I'm living in at the time is not nearly enough room for her. She needs open space to run and I think about finding another home for her. But I can't, because I want her to be a bridge to me from Kona, who is slowly dying but still alive enough to suspiciously curl her lip when Stella first arrives. I'm hoping that something in Kona will transfer to Stella like some sort of osmosis, but that process is slow in coming and I'm not sure it's happening at all, especially one morning when Stella leaves deep scratch marks down the back of one of the neighborhood kids who dares to pull her tail.

So I don't like Stella but I love her. I love her when I clean up the shredded toilet paper trail she leaves behind and pay her vet bills. I love her when I teach her in the smallest and most fleeting of moments to walk on a leash and not take down children or jump on people. I love her when I feed her and fill her water bowl. I love her in time and patience and belief and doing.

But I don't like her. Not until the night Kona dies.

Kona's head has just gone limp in my lap when my friend and I hear a rustling sound that starts outside and comes up the stairs. My friend turns to see what the noise is and her face changes from sadness to shock and I follow her gaze to see Stella clutching in her mouth the body bag intended for Kona, laboring to pull it up the stairs without stepping on it with her oversized paws. She manages to get the bag all the way up and then drags it over to Kona's body, where she gently lets the corner of the plastic fall from her mouth and looks at me and then Kona and then me again and it's a stunning moment of transition and beauty and sadness and grace all in one.

I can't believe it and I look over at my friend and her face tells me that she can't believe it either and I begin to feel everything rise up inside of me so I kiss Kona's forehead and move her head off my lap and spill down the stairs and out of the house with Stella close behind me. We run on the beach as if I can escape the loss if I run fast enough and cry hard enough and after a while I lose Stella in the coming darkness so I sit on the sand with my head in my hands, waiting for her to find me.

I feel something hit the sand between my feet and I look down through my fingers to see Stella's big brown paws on either side of a little plastic green fish she has found somewhere on the beach. My eyes are blurred from the tears as I look up at her face and her head is leaning to one side like she's trying to tell me something, but it's getting dark so I leave the fish there in the sand and we run back to the house.

Later that night as I sit drained on the floor I hear something drop to the ground next to me and again it's the little plastic green fish. I hand it back to Stella and ask her why she's carried it all the way back home but she doesn't tell me until later that night, when I make my way down this hallway for the first time in many years without my best friend at my heels.

In my room on the bed she used to share with Kona is Stella, already fast asleep. She has rarely left Kona's side in these last days and has been sleeping as close to her as possible, always touching her somehow. And now Kona is gone but Stella's front legs still seem to be wrapped around something, just like they were wrapped around Kona's fading body the night before.

Except something really is there, peeking out from the crook of Stella's front leg. My breath catches and my heart swells and there is the dog I will finally begin to like, who will soon start to win over strangers with her undefeatable spirit and love. There is my bridge.

There is Stella, her body wrapped around a little plastic green fish, her big brown paws holding on the best they can.

Stella with her head on the plastic fish,
the day after Kona dies

I'm standing at the back door in Idaho watching the late summer flies dance around Annie as she stands like a statue in the middle of her field. Soon I will see autumn leaves in the air, then snow on the ground, then the new life of spring, all from this back door. I will see the earth breathe and retreat and rejoice, I will see the sky full of lightning and fury and calm, I will see the seasons turn like so many eras in our lives, I will see it all from this back door.

But now it's the fading days of summer and I wonder what Annie is thinking out in that field. I wonder if it's a more guttural feeling and sensing of movement around her than thinking or if she has some kind of memory of moments, like the way dust falls through the light in the morning outside her shed. I wonder what she would say to me if she could.

And I wonder what Sidney would say to Brienne or Christian if he could, so I imagine what could be and write words from the horse, some kind of a response from Sidney to Brienne. But like horses and dogs and humans, we can never truly know what the other is thinking or feeling. We must trust that the real knowing is in what the other does, it is in the horse carrying the boy, it is in the dog carrying the little plastic green fish, it is in us carrying each other, helping each other rise.

*   *   *

rise

sometimes i lie awake early a.m.
and i feel that feeling come on again
the way dust settles on a river run dry

i watch as the mountain she comes alive
and the last morning star fades into light
until dark falls away from the sky

and i rise
brother i rise

i come to my door and i patiently wait

for the sound of your voice outside the gate
i know you're coming for me

we walk this road an eternal mile
the pain goes away when i feel you smile
and for now we can be free

and we rise
brother we rise
we fly
brother we fly
goodbye
goodbye

oh how we soar
oh like never before

until the day and the night turns to one
by our second turn around the sun
something beautiful has begun

when we rise
brother we rise
we fly
brother we fly
goodbye
goodbye

goodbye
we ain't ever coming down
i said we ain't ever coming down
but we always come down

sometimes i lie awake early a.m.
and i feel that feeling come on again
the way dust settles on a river run dry

*   *   *

As fall approaches Swiftsure's executive director invites me to go on a ride with her up into a different mountain pass north of town. She picks me up at the highway intersection pulling a huge stock trailer behind her truck with her family crammed into the cab and loads Annie into the trailer with the family horses. I climb into the truck with her young daughter and son and mountain man of a husband, who will be hunting off their horses while we ride.

We drive through town and into wilder country, eventually turning left off the highway up a jeep trail. We park the trailer where the road ends and unload and tack up the horses and I crawl up onto Annie. The husband says *Looks like rain* and hands me a Carhartt heavy denim jacket and within a few minutes the first drops begin to fall. We ride cross-country up the pass, sometimes on a trail and sometimes not, but either way this is hard country made of boulders and fallen trees and crevices and steep shale fields. I'm riding behind the young girl and she hangs off the saddle this way and that as if she was born in it. The whole family rides with a knowing that's bred not learned and as we approach rivers and trees and boulder crossings I watch them and mimic the way they sit and move on their horses in the hope that I'll stay in the saddle and Annie will stay upright.

We come to an incline that slopes steeper as it approaches the river and drops off a few feet above the rushing water and we have to make a hard right turn single file to avoid plunging off the edge. The young girl in front of me reaches her right leg behind her and as I watch the horse's hind hooves dig in the mud, both horse and rider begin to slide down the wet incline. The girl uses her calf but really her whole body to push her horse's flank and guide the rear of the animal around the corner while the front hooves gain enough traction to pull the rest of the horse up and out with a couple of feet to spare. There's no time to think about anything and I do the same thing I saw the girl do and Annie slides and turns and pulls out of the corner and carries me on, away, out of the pass and back to the trailer where the family comments on what a great mare I have. And as I pull her saddle off I say a quiet *Thank you* to Annie and a single-sentence prayer of gratitude to whatever may be that we aren't still trying to climb out of that river.

A few weeks later I take a trip back down to San Diego so we can record "Rise," another song we've written from Christian to Sidney called "With You," and a third I hope to finish while I'm there. Jordan and Molly and I gather in a circle around several microphones and I play the skeleton of my idea on guitar while they sing the words, but the song is still only bones with life not yet breathed into it, so we move on.

breathing life into songs

As Molly sings "With You" I close my eyes and re-play the moment of Annie and me sliding down the hill toward the river and it's her hooves gripping the loose ground, not mine, and her legs carrying us, not my own. I only move because she carries me and she also carries herself and together we are one life moving through air and leaves and rain and mud.

I open my eyes and look down at the shirt I'm wear-ing, given to me by a friend of a friend. I've already spilled coffee on it, right over the first O in the printed black ink across my chest that happens to read *Love Is The Move-ment.* I didn't mean to wear this particular shirt, taken in my barely awake haste from the pile of clothes on my dresser. But here I am, not knowing I have a shirt on that says *Love Is The Movement* and thinking about how love really is the movement. Movement made possible when one carries the other, when I move because Annie carries me away from the river, when Frank moves because Dan carries him over the rocks.

And when Christian moves because Sidney carries him to somewhere beautiful.

*   *   *

with you

carrying the burden every day
you give yourself away
in return for hope and love

The Field

is hand in hand with faith

walk this road
share this heavy load
when i'm with you
my arms are wings
my words i sing
i am everything
when i'm with you

i have always wondered if it's true
if deep inside of you

an ancient heart beats loud
and strong like the beating of a drum
walk this road
share this heavy load
when i'm with you

my arms are wings
my words i sing
i am everything
when i'm with you
i am everything
when i'm with you
i am everything
when i'm with you
i am everything

FOR THE SENDER: LOVE IS (NOT A FEELING)

when i'm with you

i have always wondered if it's true
if deep inside of you
an ancient heart beats loud and strong

*   *   *

I have come to Idaho alone but for Stella and Annie, leaving behind a gentle, caring woman who loves me in the making of sandwiches for my long airplane rides and notes left on my pillow when I come back home. I love her in my arms wrapping around her when she wants to run from her past and I love her in the lighting of the gas supply line to the fireplace when there's no wood but she's shivering so I open the valve until the flame leaps and dances warmth onto her back.

One night before I leave she's in the other room and I hear her sing just three notes in the beautiful voice that she's shy about letting anyone but me hear. They are only three notes but they feel like a hymn written on brittle paper colored in sepia tones, a hymn as old as the spirit of the horse, and I write what I hear as I sit on my couch while she's still singing those three notes. I can see a horse walking away into skies on fire that welcome a sun not yet risen and I can hear voices singing alone but together, as the sun is alone but part of the sky. This is the third song I was hoping for and one we will record live with Jordan and Molly standing around the piano, the last song with them together and an ending coda to this collection of songs about letters.

I love the woman but I still leave her and she says she'll wait. I wonder why I do this, why I continue to be drawn to this open road where the sage unfolds across the plains and the heart of the horse still beats strong under these western skies. I wonder, and I go.

*   *   *

long may you roam

in the hour before dawn
under breaking western skies
i believe you carry on
i can see with closing eyes

in the way the sun lay
upon your skin
free somehow between now
and what has been
long may you roam
long may you roam

far away from the chain
they have made to hold you in
between sage and desert rain
i believe you walk again

into light under flight
of ancient wing
all around hear the sound
of angels sing
long may you roam
long may you roam
long may you roam

*   *   *

It's the first time I've ever ridden Annie bareback and probably the first time she's ever been ridden like this and as I slowly ease down onto her from the fence rail I can feel her spine shift under me, as if I'm sitting on a bike frame, except this is no metal, man-made piece of tubing because I can feel every tensing and every releasing of every muscle in her back and it's like nothing I have ever felt before, a physical connection with something almost otherworldly in its power. There's no saddle to buffer the angles of my bones digging into her back, there are no stirrups against which to hedge her movement, there's nothing but a child who used to be a man, moving on a beast whose history is as ancient as the thunderclouds tracing from the west and the wild sky holding space for their path.

Afterward Annie is standing at the fence looking out over the valley that extends behind the field and I settle against the wood rail a few feet away from her, following her gaze. I become lost in recent moving-picture memories of her refusal to let me take space this close to her, remembering hard moments when she would throw her head and spin away to a safer place if I got too close. *At least I can stand at arm's length now* I think to myself.

The trust, the respect, and the patience have brought us here, to arm's length.

And then I feel a hot breath of air against the skin of my stomach. And then another. And another. I slowly look down and see her muzzle resting gently against the space between my jeans and my shirt, the fabric of which is caught on one of the splintering fence rails. She has walked these few steps, quietly closing the space between us to nothing and I can feel the wet of her nostrils moving in and out with her breath and the dry softness of her muzzle in between the flares. She doesn't move and neither do I.

I close my eyes and I see images as bookends and I remember that cold January night not long ago watching images as bookends from behind the theater screen. But these aren't scenes of a beginning to an end, these are scenes of the horse turning her head to bite me, to walking back to her stall after that first painful fall, to the step backward in trust, all the way up to these few soft steps across the fence rail she's just taken to be closer to me. These are different kinds of bookends.

We stand there for a long time, Annie and I. The late afternoon sky begins to fall and we are still standing there. The sun drops behind the mountain framing the house and we are still standing there. The wind takes on a twilight chill, carrying the early wet drops of the coming storm, and we are still standing there. Stella begins to bark inside the house at the first claps of thunder, and we are still standing there.

Sometimes in the moments just before I fall asleep I see a boy and a horse. They are small figures against a fence in an open field, that small field set in a deep mountain gulch, that small gulch spilling into a wide river valley under a patchwork of stars growing brighter under a darkening sky.

And we are still standing there.

Me and Annie

Love Is (Not a Feeling)

CODA *(music)*

concluding passage — It. L. cauda tail.

∪

There's a story in Native American folklore about how the Creator gave humans two companions for their journey through life: the Dog and the Horse. They called the Horse "the magic dog" and the legend says that the two-legged, four-legged, and winged creatures all lived in harmony on Earth, until one day the mischievous Coyote started telling the two-leggeds that they needed their own language.

The Creator heard the Coyote making trouble and ordered him away, but it was too late. The humans soon had their own words that only they could understand, and they began keeping secrets from the animals. They forgot the sounds of the other creatures and started hunting them, driving them deep into the forest. The Creator was angered by the humans' betrayal, and to protect the animals he sent a giant earthquake to Earth, tearing it in two. On one side would be all the animals, and on the other side the humans.

This frightened the humans to their core, because they understood that they would forever be disconnected from other creatures and eternally alone. The humans called across the widening divide to the animals, begging for forgiveness and pleading with them to jump back across the chasm. Most of the animals were so distrustful of the humans that they retreated farther back into the forest, never to truly be with them again.

Two animals heard the humans and came charging out of the forest to leap across the canyon, just as it was becoming too wide to cross: the Horse and the Dog. The humans were overjoyed and promised to always honor and respect them. The Creator told the humans to remember the choice that the Horse and the Dog made, and to never forget the special gift given to them: that gift of unconditional love embodied in their very being, the love embodied in that leap across the chasm. The love in the doing.

After that late-afternoon bareback ride on Annie I stood looking at the wall of trees that travel up from the valley floor outside my kitchen window. Many of the aspens were already changing from green to yellow to orange to brilliant red and I was reminded of an autumn not long ago when both my dreams and myself were barely hanging on, just like the leaves now in the late October wind.

My mind turned to Kona, my loyal best friend for so many years, whose ashes still sit above the couch in my living room, nestled in a box with a letter I wrote to her the day she died. And Stella, who took the torch from

Kona when she couldn't carry it anymore, a torch in the shape of a little plastic green fish. They are the Dog.

And I thought about Annie, who has already taught me deeper lessons than I could ever have imagined and guided me toward a more authentic way of living. She is the Horse.

Early the morning that Annie came into my life in California, I wrote her a letter in the form of a song. I was full of hope and uncertainty and I sat in my kitchen with my guitar, singing the letter to the music I had just written as a heavy fog clung to the Pacific Ocean outside my window. I recorded it with my phone resting on the worn wooden table and left the song there, trapped in the device, and didn't listen to it or play it again.

Until that night I rode Annie bareback. While I was standing out there with her, just as the storm was starting to leave huge, wet drops on my hat, I remembered that I'd written that song to her. The feeling was very much the same as when I was standing in my kitchen in San Diego, sorting through the lyrics, notes, and letters of the first For the Sender project. Back then I was dripping salt water from my wetsuit onto the kitchen floor when I realized that I had written my own letter to Kona the day she died.

This time, the full-circle feeling was the same, but now I was standing in my kitchen in Idaho, dripping rainwater on the floor. And instead of reading a letter of remembering, I was reading one of hope.

That letter to Kona had closed a chapter.
This letter opened one.

*   *   *

dear annie

dear annie
i can't believe
you're coming to me
i dreamt you running
long before i knew your name
dear annie
did you dream the same

dear annie
you're a wing and a prayer
out a field somewhere
you came from a southern sunrise
on a missouri breeze
dear annie
i hope i make you happy

you came from a southern sunrise
on a missouri breeze
and I'm going to love you
deep as the next winter's freeze
dear annie
i hope i make you happy

*   *   *

Annie stood just outside the front window in the rain, grazing on the last standing blades of autumn grass. Night had fallen fast and in the reflection of the kitchen window I again saw the jumbled flash of scenes I'd just seen out in the field: my face in the dirt, her rigid glares, broken body parts and mended hearts for both of us. I saw an entire progression of mistrust moving to trust, impatience moving to patience, disrespect moving to respect.

I saw other scenes too, scenes passing by in parentheses like they shared the same beginning, all interchangeable as part of the same sentence. I saw (my dad walking across the kitchen to my mom) (Dan carrying Frank over the rocks) (the care that's bringing my Grandma back) (Jesse taking a bullet and Scarlett shining a light) (the teacher reaching for his daughter as she sings for him) (my dad picking me up from school) (Loren watching Graham at the show and at my house) (the horse unmoving on top of the little girl) (Sidney carrying Christian) (Annie carrying me).

These scenes had nothing to do with some fog of attribution or nebular sense of beauty or wanting or thinking or longing to do. They were about the real doing, being, moving, the real taking of a step across a chasm or a rock or a room, the taking of a step backward in trust and forward in love. And I realized that in every scene was an answer to a need. A choice. To me that's what love is. Not a feeling.

My attention turned from the window to a search for "Dear Annie" on my phone. I was worried that I'd deleted it by accident but found it buried among other song ideas, and as I listened to it I noticed how I asked Annie if she somehow found me, if she dreamt me, just as I found her. Maybe she was out there in that field somewhere long before I knew her, standing not with romantic love but with something that can't be manipulated or manufactured or lost. Maybe everything she stood for was forged by patience and respect and trust and she was just looking for the same thing in somebody. Like we all are.

I watched her take a few slow strides away from the window and out of the frame and thought about how not everybody wants a dog or a horse or a cat or a bird or anything besides themselves that they have to take care of. But I hope people eventually find that kind of connection somewhere, because there are lessons of accountability and authenticity and love in those relationships. And honesty. As far as I can tell, animals don't really know how to lie or be lied to.

And maybe one reason so many people do love their animals, sometimes more than the humans in their lives, is because love is inherent in keeping them alive, woven into seemingly simple acts like giving food and water. Love isn't separate from the act, it is the act, born in the smallest decision to do something.

I turned off the kitchen lights and headed down the hall for bed with a small smile. Even though that song starts off "Dear Annie," I didn't write it for her. She didn't hear the song back then, still hasn't heard it, and, being a horse, wouldn't understand the words if she did hear it. And it wouldn't matter, because like the other songs about letters that we wrote and recorded, and like the letters themselves, that one to Annie was more for the sender. It still is.

And I do believe in that Native American myth about the Horse and the Dog, same as I believe in the story of Jesus, because the truths those stories represent are so deep, so proven, so true, that to believe in the story is to believe in its reality. Our ancestors and those before them told these stories, and many others, for a reason.

They are true.

THANKS

to these special people for their talent and support

Wendy Laister
Orla Clarke
Libby Lyman
Debra White
Cheryl Bennett
Tonya Hamilton
Amanda Johnson
Nick Ortner
Barbara Dembergh
Caroline Woodham
Nena Anderson
Stefanie Bond
Carina Sammartino
Lee Sammartino
Dr. Wayne Dyer

Jordan Pundik
Molly Jenson
Jack Tempchin
Graham Nancarrow
Skye Dyer
Patrick McClory
Deane Cote
Isaac Marr
Dan Bailey
Rami Jaffe
David Thoener
Reid Tracy
Margarete Nielsen
Nancy Levin
Coleman Barks

And Dan, Scarlett, Loren, Serena, and Brienne

MUSIC CREDITS

Breathe The Sky
Written by Alex Woodard and Jordan Pundik
Published by Woodshack Music (ASCAP) / The Real Prune Balloon (BMI)
/ Dean Allen Cote (BMI)

Never Let You Go
Written by Alex Woodard
Published by Woodshack Music (ASCAP)

There's No Goodbye
Written by Alex Woodard and Jack Tempchin
Published by Woodshack Music (ASCAP) / Night River Publishing
(ASCAP)

Bullet
Written by Alex Woodard
Published by Woodshack Music (ASCAP)

So You Would Know
Written by Alex Woodard and Jordan Pundik
Published by Woodshack Music (ASCAP) / The Real Prune Balloon (BMI)
/ Dean Allen Cote (BMI)

Celebration (Scarlett's Song)
Written by Alex Woodard and Molly Jenson
Published by Woodshack Music (ASCAP) / Wally Jay Music (ASCAP)

We Ain't Got The Time
Written by Alex Woodard and Graham Nancarrow
Published by Woodshack Music (ASCAP)

This Gift
Recorded live at Escondido Center for the Arts, September 25, 2013
Written by Alex Woodard
Published by Woodshack Music (ASCAP)

Who I Come From
Written by Alex Woodard
Published by Woodshack Music (ASCAP)

Rise
Written by Alex Woodard and Jordan Pundik
Published by Woodshack Music (ASCAP) / The Real Prune Balloon (BMI)
/ Dean Allen Cote (BMI)

With You
Written by Alex Woodard and Molly Jenson
Published by Woodshack Music (ASCAP) / Wally Jay Music (ASCAP)

Long May You Roam
Written by Alex Woodard
Published by Woodshack Music (ASCAP)

Dear Annie
Written by Alex Woodard
Published by Woodshack Music (ASCAP)

Produced by Alex Woodard
Mixed by David Thoener
Mastered by Andrew Mendelson at Georgetown Masters

ABOUT THE AUTHOR

When he's not surfing in a little beach town north of San Diego, Alex lives with a big dog and a bigger horse in the mountains of Idaho.

Please visit www.AlexWoodard.com
to learn more.

∪

If you'd like to have your own
handwritten letter
considered for a song, please mail it to:

For The Sender
c/o Hay House
P.O. Box 5100
Carlsbad, CA 92018

While a song can't be written about every letter, we do
read them all. Please be sure to include your contact
information so we can reach out to you if necessary.

We hope you enjoyed this Hay House book. If you'd like to receive our online catalog featuring additional information on Hay House books and products, or if you'd like to find out more about the Hay Foundation, please contact:

Hay House, Inc., P.O. Box 5100, Carlsbad, CA 92018-5100
(760) 431-7695 or (800) 654-5126
(760) 431-6948 *(fax)* or (800) 650-5115 *(fax)*
www.hayhouse.com® • www.hayfoundation.org

***

Published and distributed in Australia by: Hay House Australia Pty. Ltd., 18/36 Ralph St., Alexandria NSW 2015 • *Phone: 612-9669-4299* Fax: 612-9669-4144 • www.hayhouse.com.au

Published and distributed in the United Kingdom by: Hay House UK, Ltd., Astley House, 33 Notting Hill Gate, London W11 3JQ • *Phone: 44-20-3675-2450* • *Fax: 44-20-3675-2451* www.hayhouse.co.uk

Published and distributed in the Republic of South Africa by: Hay House SA (Pty), Ltd., P.O. Box 990, Witkoppen 2068 • *Phone/Fax:* 27-11-467-8904 • www.hayhouse.co.za

Published in India by: Hay House Publishers India, Muskaan Complex, Plot No. 3, B-2, Vasant Kunj, New Delhi 110 070 *Phone: 91-11-4176-1620* • *Fax: 91-11-4176-1630* • www.hayhouse.co.in

Distributed in Canada by: Raincoast Books, 2440 Viking Way, Richmond, B.C. V6V 1N2 • *Phone: 1-800-663-5714* *Fax: 1-800-565-3770* • www.raincoast.com